THE FRENCH NEW TOWNS

JOHNS HOPKINS STUDIES IN URBAN AFFAIRS

Center for Metropolitan Planning and Research
The Johns Hopkins University

David Harvey, *Social Justice and the City*
Ann L. Strong, *Private Property and the Public Interest: The Brandywine Experience*
Alan D. Anderson, *The Origin and Resolution of an Urban Crisis: Baltimore, 1890–1930*
James M. Rubenstein, *The French New Towns*

THE FRENCH NEW TOWNS

James M. Rubenstein

THE JOHNS HOPKINS UNIVERSITY PRESS
Baltimore and London

The Johns Hopkins University Press, Baltimore, Maryland 21218
The Johns Hopkins Press Ltd., London

Library of Congress Catalog Card Number 77–26953 ISBN 0–8018–2104–5

Library of Congress Cataloging in Publication data will be found on the last printed page of this book.

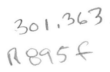

To my parents, with love and gratitude

CONTENTS

FIGURES

TABLES

TERMS AND ABBREVIATIONS

AFTRP Agence Foncière et Technique de la Région Parisienne (Paris region land development agency), a governmental agency created in 1962 to acquire land in the Paris region for public purposes and to equip it with any needed infrastructure. In the early days of the new towns, AFTRP was the only agency in the Paris region that had the authority to begin developing the new towns sites.

CDC Caisse des Dépôts et Consignations (national bank), a nationally owned and operated bank that serves as the most important financial institution in France. It receives its funds from individual depositers who save through their local post offices. The CDC plays two important roles. First, it is the main source of loans to local authorities in France. Second, it regulates the nation's monetary policies through its widespread interests in a variety of projects and funds. It controls or funds a large number of special-purpose agencies and investment funds.

CDUC Commission Départemental d'Urbanisme Commercial (departmental commission for urban commercial activities), a commission established at the departmental level to approve the location of new shopping centers. The commissions consist of twenty members: nine local officials, nine local businessmen, and two consumer representatives. They have effectively limited the proliferation of small-scale shopping centers in France in recent years.

CGP Commissariat Général du Plan d'Equipement et de la Productivité (national planning commission), a government agency, created in 1946, to develop the five-year national plans for new investment. The CGP is an interministerial agency designed to coordinate the policies of the individual ministeries with regard to long-term investments. The sixth national plan (1971–75) was the first to provide a large-scale commitment to the new towns, a commitment that has been continued in the seventh plan (1976–80).

CODER Commission de Développement Economique Régional (regional commission for economic development), a consultative body at the regional level, including local councillors, technical experts, and representatives of various interest groups. The CODER advises the regional prefect concerning appropriate regional investment policies.

Communes (French local governments). There are approximately 38,000 communes in France. They are administered by an elected mayor and municipal council.

Crédit Foncier (land bank). The Crédit Foncier, founded in 1852, is the chief source of loans to private developers for housing construction. It is privately owned but has a government-appointed director. The Crédit Foncier is the most important source in France of funds for *aidé* housing, designed for middle-income families.

DAT Département d'Aménagement du Territoire (department for regional planning), a now defunct agency within the now defunct Ministry of Construction. It was the forerunner of the DATAR in the 1950s.

DATAR Délégation à l'Aménagement du Territoire et à l'Action Régionale (delegation for regional planning), the agency primarily responsible for the formulation and implementation of regional planning policies at the national level. The DATAR, formed in 1963, reviews the investment policies of the individual ministries to assure coordination of efforts to promote the provinces in France. The DATAR strongly discourages further concentration in the Paris region although it does support the Paris new towns policy.

DDE Direction Départemental d'Equipement (representatives of the Ministry of Equipment at the departmental level). The important ministries maintain cadres of civil servants in the departments to assure that national policies are being implemented at the local level. The DDE makes most decisions at the departmental level concerning investment in new roads, sewers, and other infrastructures. It is also responsible for issuing building permits.

Département (the middle level of local government in France). The department is headed by the prefect. In contrast to the situation in the communes the departmental officials are appointed by the national government, not locally elected. Consequently, the departments are not true local governments; they are largely local representatives of the national government.

EPA Etablissement Public d'Aménagement (development corporation), a special agency created to manage the development of the new towns. Unlike the British development corporation, the EPA is limited in its scope of authority. It is concerned with conducting the planning studies for the new town and in buying, equipping, and selling or leasing land in the new town. There is one EPA for each new town.

FDES Fonds de Développement Economique et Social (economic and social development fund), a fund managed by the ministry of finance, with the consultation of other national ministries and agencies. FDES invests in the nationalized industries and other projects considered of high priority according to the national plan.

FIAT Fonds d'Intervention pour l'Aménagement du Territoire (fund for regional planning assistance), a fund managed by the DATAR. The DATAR selects for investment certain projects that have not been funded by the usual sources. These projects are chosen consistent with the DATAR's overall mission of promoting the development of provinces as opposed to the Paris region.

FNAFU Fonds National d'Aménagement Foncier et de l'Urbanisme (national fund for land development and planning). FNAFU is a government agency funded by the CDC. It makes loans available to local authorities for land acquisition and site preparation in projects considered in the national interest. The loans are normally made directly to the developer, which is usually some sort of joint public-private organization in these projects of national interest. The loans, however, must be guaranteed by the communes.

GCVN Groupe Central des Villes Nouvelles (central group for new towns), an intergovernmental agency responsible for overall coordination of the new towns policy. The GCVN is the major source of data concerning the new towns. It is managed by a board of representatives from the various ministries concerned with new town development.

HLM Habitation Loyer Modérée (moderate rent housing), the government program under which the lowest cost housing is built in France. Non-profit or private organizations receive one percent loans from the government in order to build housing. The rents in the projects are set at the level needed to cover only building costs. Virtually all of this housing is in high-rise rental units, although in recent years some detached and owner-occupied low cost projects have been attempted.

IAURP Institut d'Aménagement et d'Urbanisme de la Région Parisienne (Paris regional planning agency). Created in 1960, the IAURP is the agency responsible for the development of master plans in the Paris region, including the 1965 plan, which first proposed the new towns. It is now known as the Institut d'Aménagement et d'Urbanisme de la Région d'Ile de France (IAURIF).

MEA Mission d'Etudes et d'Aménagement (planning and research commission), the first planning organization established in the new towns. When the new town site is first designated, an MEA is established to conduct the initial planning studies. Eventually, the MEA is dissolved in favor of the EPA, which has all of the MEA's functions plus the ability to buy and prepare land.

PADOG Plan d'Aménagement et d'Organisation Générale de la Région Parisienne (plan for development and general organization of the Paris region). A plan for the Paris region written in 1960, it proved to be quickly obsolete and was replaced in 1965 by the SDAU which first proposed the new towns.

PDUI Plan Directeur d'Urbanisme Intercommunaux (detailed land use plan for a multicommunal group). The PDUI is a land use plan for rural communes. It is designed to provide a relatively stable picture of the land use patterns and likely modifications in the rural areas.

POS Plan d'Occupation des Sols (detailed land use plans), land use plans for already urbanized areas. Like the PDUI, the POS is designed to provide well-planned modifications to an otherwise stable situation. Neither the PDUI nor the POS can be written for rapidly growing areas such as the new towns. In either case, the detailed plans must be consistent with SDAU.

SCA Syndicat Communautaire d'Aménagement (syndicate for community development), a collection of local governments within the territory of the new towns. The concerned communes are combined into the SCA so that only one local government will represent the new town. The SCA acts as one commune only to the extent of establishing a uniform tax base within the territory to be developed as the new town (the ZAN). The existing communes have the choice of selecting an SCA or on Ensemble Urbain. With the Ensemble Urbain the old communes disappear altogether and one new commune is formed. Only Le Vaudreuil among the French new towns has chosen the Ensemble Urbain.

SCET Société Centrale pour l'Equipement du Territoire (central corporation for land development), an agency created by the CDC to provide financial assistance to developers.

SCIC Société Centrale Immobilière de la Caisse des Dépôts (central building corporation), a building company managed by the Caisse des

Dépôts et Consignations. It was responsible for the construction of many large suburban housing estates in France, using money from SCET.

SDAU   Schéma Directeur d'Aménagement et d'Urbanisme (master plan), a long-term development plan that sets overall goals for a particular area but does not specify the exact location of new investments within the area. The master plan for the Paris region is known as the SDAURP.

SEM   Société d'économie mixte (semipublic corporation), an organization created by local authorities to manage development of new projects. It is similar to the EPA in concept but has much more limited power. The SEM is limited to activities explicitly delegated by the local authority and is considered too inflexible an organization to guide the development of a large-scale project like a new town.

SIVOM   Syndicat Intercommunal à Vocations Multiples (multipurpose union of communes), an organization created by agreement of several local authorities to establish priorities for new projects in the area and to distribute the financial obligations among the concerned communes.

SRE   Service Régionale d'Equipement (representatives of the Ministry of Equipment at the regional level). The SRE consists of civil servants who are assigned to the regions of France in order to assure that the national policies are implemented at the regional level and to provide technical assistance to the regions.

VRTS   Versement Représentatif de la Taxe sur la Salaire (revenue sharing), a payroll tax paid by employers and collected by the national government. The state then allocated the money to localities according to the two criteria of population and local tax effort. In the Paris region a special redistribution called the Fond d'Egalisation des Charges (FEC) is also used. The FEC allocates the money according to population, local tax effort, and local income.

ZAC   Zone d'Aménagement Concerté (concerted development zone). The ZAC is a contract between a local authority or EPA and a private developer concerning the distribution of costs of development for a new residential or nonresidential project. The national government makes grants and loans for infrastructure on a top priority basis. The new towns are divided into a number of ZAC's in order to permit the EPA to maintain overall development control while bringing private developers into the process on a profitable basis.

ZAD   Zone d'Aménagement Différé (deferred development zone). an area established by government decree within which prices of land are frozen at the level of one year prior to the decree. The ZAD technique is used to discourage speculation as well as to keep prices low for land to be acquired. It has been used quite liberally in the new towns.

ZAN   Zone d'Agglomération Nouvelle (new local government zone). The ZAN is the area of concern of the SCA. It is the territory over which construction for the new town will occur.

ZUP   Zone à Urbaniser en Priorité (priority development zone), a technique used widely in the 1960s, now largely superseded by the ZAC. The ZUP was an area developed by a local authority and a private developer, with top priority for national grants and loans.

ACKNOWLEDGMENTS

Research activity in a foreign country will succeed only with a substantial contribution from one's hosts. Many people in France provided invaluable assistance to me in this study. First, I would like to thank Claude Rickard of the Groupe Central des Villes Nouvelles for his many kindnesses. I would like to thank all the Fellows from the Johns Hopkins International Fellowship Program, who over the years have been extremely generous to me with both their expertise and hospitality. I would expecially like to thank the following Fellows: Michel Carmona, Didier Chartier, Jean-Raymond Fradin, Jean-Louis Husson, Michel Maillard, Max Stern, and Jean-Claude Toubon. Without their cooperation during my trips to France in 1974 and 1977 nothing would have been accomplished. Many other people in France have been extremely helpful, too numerous to mention, especially at the Institut d'Aménagement et d'Urbanisme de la Région d'Ile de France (IAURIF), the Groupe Central des Villes Nouvelles, and in the various new towns. I would like to thank Miami University for its generous support of my effort. Donna Rosenbaum of Miami University has created the maps in this book. Finally, I thank Jack C. Fisher, Director of the Center for Metropolitan Planning and Research at The Johns Hopkins University for his unbounded faith in me.

THE FRENCH NEW TOWNS

INTRODUCTION

New towns are being built as a matter of public policy around the world. In "advanced" industrial countries, in socialist Eastern Europe, and in the Third World, new towns have been selected as a relevant tool for coping with problems of urban growth. In the United States, urban policy makers have flirted with the new towns concept on several occasions, most notably with the Greenbelt towns of the 1930s and the Title VII new towns of the early 1970s. However, new towns have generally been dismissed as inappropriate and impractical for the American situation.[1]

A revitalized new towns program in the United States will only arise if fresh evidence is available to demonstrate the benefits of them. The crippled Title VII new towns can be usefully studied, but more valuable lessons may be drawn from countries where new towns programs are receiving strong government support. A considerable amount of information has been generated about the British new towns program.[2] The consensus among U.S. planners and policy makers is that the British new towns are rather successful but have limited applicablility to the American situation.

American observers who have dismissed the British experience as irrelevant to U.S. planning problems would do well to consider the French new towns program. The French have only recently turned to new towns: the first government document in support of them appeared in 1965, while large-scale construction dates from around 1970. The French program, however, more than makes up for its tardiness by the scale of the effort. The French new towns program is

[1] See, for example, William Alonso, "What Are New Towns For?," *Urban Studies* 7 (1970), and Lloyd Rodwin, *The British New Towns Policy* (Cambridge, Mass.: Harvard University Press, 1956).

[2] Among the many sources of information on British new towns are J. B. Cullingworth, *Town and Country Planning in England and Wales* (London: George Allen and Unwin, 1970); Hazel Evans, ed., *New Towns: The British Experience* (London: Charles Knight and Company, 1972); Frederic Osborn and Arnold Whittick, *The New Towns: The Answer to Megalopolis* (London: L. Hall, 1963); Frank Schaffer, *The New Towns Story* (London: MacGibbon and Fee, 1970); and *Town and Country Planning* magazine.

1

now one of the largest in the world in terms of housing starts and new employment. By the late 1970s, the French new towns were creating around 20,000 housing starts and 15,000 new jobs per year.[3]

Nine so-called "villes nouvelles" are being built in France at the moment (fig. I–1).[4] Five of the new towns are located in the Paris region: Cergy-Pontoise, located 25 kilometers northwest of central Paris; Evry, 25 kilometers south; Marne-la-Vallée, 10 kilometers to the east; Melun-Sénart, 35 kilometers southeast; and Saint-Quentin-en-Yvelines, 30 kilometers southwest. Four new towns are under construction elsewhere in France. L'Etang de Berre, 15 kilometers northwest of Marseille; Lille-Est, 5 kilometers east of Lille; L'Isle d'Abeau, 35 kilometers east of Lyon; and Le Vaudreuil, 25 kilometers southeast of Rouen. The French new towns are planned on a large scale. When completed near the end of the century, the nine new towns are expected to contain nearly three million residents. The planned sizes range from 140,000 for Le Vaudreuil to 500,000 for Evry and Berre. The others are expected to be around 250,000–300,000 each.[5]

Despite the size and expense of the French new towns, no evaluations have yet been undertaken. Data is relatively scarce, while the literature has been confined to descriptions of the physical plans or the administrative structure. Virtually nothing of significance has appeared in English. The purpose of this book is to inform planners and policy makers around the world about the French new towns. This book will analyze what the French new towns are trying to accomplish; the administrative, financial, and political reforms needed to secure implementation of the program; and the achievements of the new towns. At all times, the evaluation of the French new towns will be undertaken with an eye to international applicability.

Why build new towns? In view of the low priority given to the development of a new towns construction program in the United States, the first chapter of this study will examine the reasons for the adoption of a new towns policy in France. New towns are used to

[3] By comparison, the British new towns added 47,793 new jobs and 21,788 dwellings in 1974. Annual statistics are published in *Town and Country Planning*, usually the February issue.

[4] Several other projects in France could qualify as new towns in the broad sense of the term, including Mourenx, Toulouse-le-Mirail, and Herouville-Saint-Cair. However, these projects are not included in the structure of administration and financing that has been established by the government for the nine new towns referred to here. These are the nine "villes nouvelles." For a description of the other projects, see Pierre Merlin, *Les Villes nouvelles* (Paris: Presses Universitaires de France, 1969).

[5] The French have not established precise figures concerning the desired populations at the completion of the projects. These figures represent the approximate targets for the year 2000.

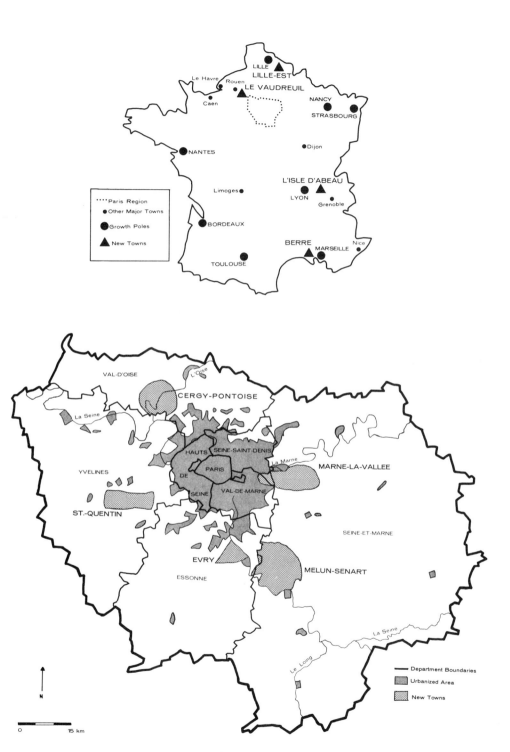

Figure I–1. The French new towns

implement national policies for managing urban and regional growth. They play two roles: they are tools of intraregional planning, by organizing the growth of metropolitan areas, and they are tools of interregional planning, by stimulating the development of relatively poor regions.

The contemporary international planning movement for the construction of new towns originated with an Englishman, Ebenezer Howard, who wrote *Garden Cities of To-Morrow*.[6] Howard called for the construction of new towns, or garden cities, on the periphery of existing urban areas. The garden city was an isolated, self-contained community planned to be a predetermined size. It represented a "marriage" between town and country, where residents enjoy both the employment and shopping opportunities of the city and the healthy environment of the countryside. Surrounding the town would be a green belt of permanent open space to prevent sprawl and to preserve the physical independence of the garden city. The population would be recruited from overcrowded existing cities, to enable their redevelopment at lower densities. Once the planned size of 32,000 was reached, the garden city would no longer grow; further regional growth would be concentrated in additional new towns. Eventually, a system of new towns would be developed, each physically separated by a green belt but linked by a transportation system.

Howard's book, written in 1898, literally as well as symbolically marked the culmination of nineteenth-century concern for the implications of rapid urbanization. Nineteenth-century cities were characterized by poor physical and social conditions. Residents in the rapidly growing cities suffered from diseases and a high mortality rate. Health problems were aggravated by poverty. Wages were low and unemployment high. Housing was overcrowded and without running water or adequate ventilation. Crime and other social disorders increased. The factories produced smoke and other pollutants.

Mumford has said, "Perhaps the greatest contribution made by the industrial town was the reaction it produced against its own greatest misdemeanors."[7] Three types of reactions to the poor physical conditions in the nineteeth-century cities can be detected: (1) to "tinker" with existing cities by installing water and sewer systems,

[6]Cambridge, Mass., and London: The M.I.T. Press, 1965. Originally published in 1898 as *To-Morrow: A peaceful Path to Real Reform*.

[7]Lewis Mumford, *The City in History* (New York: Harcourt, Brace and Company, 1961).

slum clearance, highway construction, etc.; (2) to build suburbs that permit workers to escape from urban conditions every evening; and (3) to construct entirely new towns without the poor conditions of existing cities. The first two movements attracted the attention of most urban reformers, but it is the third one that concerns this book.

In recent years, new towns have played an additional role in the development of national urban growth policies. Planners concerned with the disparities between the richer and poorer parts of the country have sought ways to reduce the gap. The poorer regions suffer from relatively depressed economies characterized by high unemployment and declining industries. To improve the economic conditions in the depressed regions, new jobs must be located there. However, different jobs have different impacts on the region's economic development. Jobs in certain industries will stimulate more economic growth than others. Some economists call these industries "basic" industries, because they sell most of their products outside the region and consequently bring in money. These industries contrast with "nonbasic" or "service" industries, which serve only the local population and merely recirculate money within the locality. Other economists call the key firms "propulsive" industries. The addition of a propulsive industry to a region will stimulate demand for other firms that sell products to the propulsive industry. Growth-inducing industries increase the demand for a variety of supporting services and facilities, such as housing, schools, shops, and recreation for the new workers.

New towns have been constructed in connection with these growth-inducing industries. Such towns provide the most up-to-date services and facilities for the convenience of the new industries. New towns can also be used directly to stimulate regional development. If propulsive industries can not easily be attracted, employment opportunities can be provided in the region by the construction of a new town. New towns can be the focus of investment in a depressed region where the existing urban areas are considered unattractive. Given this theoretical understanding of the intra- and interregional roles of new towns in the development of national urban growth policies, Chapter 1 will examine the reasons why new towns are now being built in France.

Chapter 2 is concerned with the administrative structure by which new towns are built in France. American critics invariably cite the need for administrative reform as a fundamental reason for the infeasibility of the new towns idea in the United States. Local authority boundaries are inappropriate for solving urban problems but are unlikely to be changed in the near future. New towns require a higher degree of coordination among different governments than is currently exercised in the United States. Pessimism expressed by American writers concerning the practical ability to create new towns within the American administrative system is used as an excuse for evoking generally negative attitudes toward new towns. The critics may be correct about the likelihood of fundamental change in the American legal structure but they are wrong in their assessment of the extent of administrative reform actually needed. The belief that a unique form of administrative structure must be created in order to build new towns is based on knowledge of only the British new towns administration.

The British have a simple administrative structure for developing new towns. Each town is directed by a development corporation, appointed by the national government, that carries out virtually all aspects of urban development. It prepares the master plan, buys the land, installs roads and utilities, builds structures, rents the buildings and acts as landlord or sells them, provides maintenance, builds parks and playgrounds, provides the shopping centers and pubs, runs the buses, etc. Existing local authorities are consulted as a matter of courtesy but have little impact on policy decisions.

Critics who consider new towns impractical in the United States because the British administrative structure for creating them could never be adopted should examine the French experience. Like the United States, France has a large number of small local authorities with legal responsibility in the urban development process. In fact, France has fifty percent more local authorities per capita than the United States. The territory of the nine new towns encompasses 114 local governments. French planners have demonstrated that, given the will at the national level, an effective new towns policy can be developed with minimal changes in the traditional governmental structure.

The third chapter concentrates on major economic questions associated with new towns. The British method of financing new towns has been much admired but not replicated in other democratic societies. The British development corporation receives fifty-year Treasury loans to pay for construction costs. It must demonstrate that the project is likely to be financially sound. If the Treasury is satisfied with the financial prospects, it makes the loan at a rate of interest comparable to the rates available to other prime borrowers. The loans are repaid with the assets received by the development corporation primarily through sale or leasing of land or structures. This system gives the corporation a good deal of independence because it is freed from the need to secure capital grants on an annual basis.

Neither the French nor the American new towns have been able to secure the degree of financial independence enjoyed by the British.

The United States attempted to solve the problem by providing loan guarantees to private developers. A developer who wished to build a new town applied to the Department of Housing and Urban Development (HUD) for a guarantee of up to $50 million to facilitate borrowing money from private financial sources at a lower rate of interest than would otherwise be available. In return the developer had to work for certain social and physical planning goals. The $50 million limit on guarantees to each new town proved inadequate when the U.S. economy slowed in the early 1970s. House sales lagged, reducing the rate of income generation. New towns developers, who were inexperienced with working at such a large scale, were unable to meet their financial targets. As a result HUD has had to provide more grants and guarantees than anticipated. In the long run, the new towns may still be profitable. At this time, however, they have required a larger government contribution than expected.

The French have steered a middle course between the monolithic national government framework in Great Britain and the dike-stopping approach of the American government. It is a complex system, heavily influenced by French administration irrationalities, and many problems remain. Although numerous difficulties have arisen, the system has been sufficiently workable to recommend it for analysis by the international planning community.

Chapter 4 discusses the role of the private sector in the French new towns development process. In Great Britain, the public sector performs virtually all the tasks associated with the building of the new towns, while the American new towns are almost entirely private ventures. Private developers are strongly involved in the French new towns effort, but the division of responsibilities between the public and private sectors is more rational in France than that achieved in the United States under the Title VII program. The French government in effect acts as the prime developer for the new towns, assuming most of the financial risks. The large new town sites are divided into smaller units, which are manageable by private developers. This arrangement avoids one of the major problems in the American new towns program. In the United States, new towns have been too large for private developers to manage successfully with their existing methods. The French have recognized the fact that private involvement is most efficient if the private developers are permitted to work at their more usual scale of operations. Consequently, the government has devised a number of tools to channel private developers into the new towns and away from undesirable locations.

Chapter 5 examines the major accomplishment of the French new towns: the achievement of socially balanced communities. In contrast to most one-class dormitory suburbs, the new towns contain a relatively heterogeneous population, with a mixture of working-class and middle-class families. Furthermore, the new towns are planned to achieve a balance between residences and nonresidential functions, particularly employment opportunities. Many European cities, including Paris, are socially segregated in a spatial pattern different from U.S. cities—the poor live in the periphery rather than the center. Despite these differences the social problem is basically the same: geographic segregation prevents the poor from achieving access to the high quality of housing and supporting services enjoyed by the middle class. Because of their peripheral location the French new towns run the risk of being all low-income projects. Planners have therefore placed a high priority on the attraction of middle-income families to ensure a balanced mix of social classes. This policy has achieved considerable success. Middle-class families have been attracted through the provision of single-family, owner-occupied housing, good shops and recreation facilities, and especially through the provision of job opportunities, including offices.

In the United States new towns have been proposed as a mechanism for integrating low-income families into suburbs that are otherwise closed to them. The French experience demonstrates that socially heterogeneous new communities can be developed, even within the framework of a market system, if a sufficiently high priority is placed on the effort.

For the American observer, two broad patterns emerged in evaluating the achievements of the French new towns. First, the French managed to overcome considerable political and financial obstacles to implement the new towns program. In particular, the French planners had to face problems relating to the inclusion of local authorities and the private sector in the development process. Their solution is extremely relevant to American problems of urban development. Second, the benefits from building new towns are more in the field of social planning than physical planning. The French new towns, like similar programs elsewhere in the world, have not been able to capture the percentage of growth planned for the regions where they are located. However, this study concludes that new towns appear to provide a measurably superior way of life for its residents than is available in alternative forms of urban growth.

1
THE NEW TOWNS IDEA

The current new towns effort in France can be traced back to the 1965 master plan for the Paris region, called the Schéma Directeur d'Aménagement et d'Urbanisme de la Région de Paris (SDAURP). [1] The SDAURP was the first official document in France to propose the construction of new towns. It called for the accommodation of most of the Paris region's growth in eight peripheral new towns, which would range in size from 400,000 to 1,000,000 residents by the year 2000. These eight new towns would be located along two development corridors, or preferential axes. The axes were designed to run parallel courses from southeast to northwest, tangent to the north and south sides of the existing built-up area (see fig. 1–1). Three new towns were proposed for the northern axis and five for the southern. Along the north side, the existing suburban areas of Saint-Denis, Sarcelles, and Bobigny were to be extended to the west to new towns at Beauchamp and Pontoise. To the east the axis would include the new airport at Roissy, the redevelopment of the soon to be abandoned Le Bourget Airport as a new employment and shopping center, and the new town of Noisy-le-Grand. Along the south side, five new towns were planned. Three were included west of Versailles—two at Trappes and one at Mantes. Evry was planned near Orly Airport and the Rungis industrial area (the site of the transplanted Les Halles market). Further east, a large new town called Tigery-Lieusaint was programmed for the area south of the forest of Sénart and north of Melun.

Of the eight new towns proposed in the SDAURP, five are now under construction: Cergy-Pontoise and Marne-la-Vallée (formerly Noisy-le-Grand) along the northern axis and Saint-Quentin-en-Yve-

---

[1] Délégué General au District de la Région de Paris, *Schéma Directeur de l'aménagement et d'urbanisme de la région parisienne*, 3 vols. (Paris: Délégation Général de la Région de Paris, 1966). The SDAURP was revised in 1975.

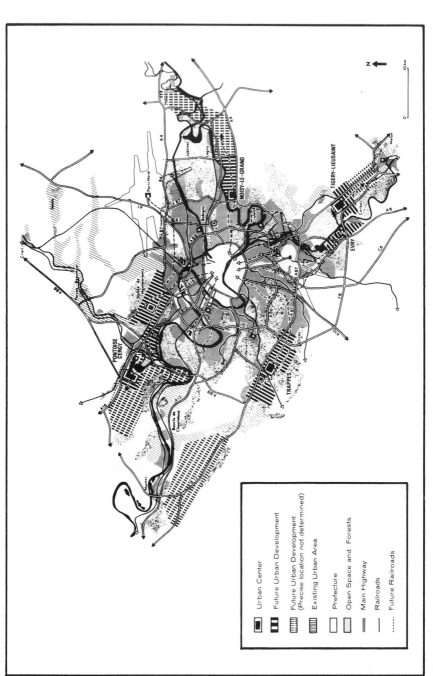

Figure 1–1. The Paris region master plan of 1965. Eight new towns were proposed along two axes tangential to the existing built-up area. Compare this plan with the modifications adopted in 1969 (figure 1–2). (Préfecture de la Région Parisienne, *La Région parisienne: quatre années d'aménagement et d'équipement* [Paris: Institut d'Aménagement at d'Urbanisme de la Région Parisienne, 1973], p. 8)

Urban Center

Future Urban Development

Future Urban Development
(Precise location not determined)

Existing Urban Area

Prefecture

Open Space and Forests

Main Highway

Railroads

Future Railroads

lines (formerly Trappes), Evry, and Melun-Sénart (formerly Tigery-Lieusaint) along the southern axis. Two of the proposed towns were eliminated because of strong opposition from local officials, while Saint-Quentin-en-Yvelines combined two sites into one (fig. 1–2). These five new towns are designed to accommodate around 1.7 million people by 2000 rather than the original 4.5 million.

While the Paris regional planners were advocating the construction of new towns, the national planners in the DATAR were also attracted to the idea. Studies carried out in the three *métropoles d'équilibres* of Lille, Lyon, and Marseille indicated that regional growth would have to take place outside the existing urbanized area. For various reasons new towns were recommended at these *métropoles*. In the Lille region, a new town was needed to provide services and facilities for a large university complex being built to the east of the city. At Lyon, two new towns were proposed to counteract the tendency of the Lyon suburbs to sprawl in all directions. These were located on the east side of Lyon in order to preserve vineyards and other natural amenities elsewhere in the region and to strengthen the development of axes between Lyon and Grenoble, Chambéry, and Annecy. One of the two new towns, L'Isle d'Abeau, has been started adjacent to a new airport that will be one of the largest in France.

The new town at Marseille was necessitated by the decision to increase the port capacity. Because large-scale expansion was blocked at the existing port area, an entirely new port is being built on the Gulf of Fos, to the west of Marseille. The adjacent new town of Berre will provide the needed supporting services for the port facilities. A fourth new town is Le Vaudreuil, near Rouen. It will help to organize the large-scale growth anticipated in the Basse-Seine corridor, which extends from Paris to the English Channel at Le Havre. The new town is designed to prevent this growth from occurring in a sprawling extension from Paris by channeling development into the new town well beyond the current limits of the Paris region.

THE FAILURE OF NEW TOWNS IN THE UNITED STATES AND THEIR SUCCESS IN GREAT BRITAIN

In the United States business and social reformers have long toyed with the new towns idea. Yet U.S. efforts until 1970 have remained isolated and uncoordinated, with one exception outside the concern of the government — the Greenbelt towns constructed during the 1930s. Three new towns were developed by the Resettlement Administration under the leadership of Rex Tugwell: Greenbelt,

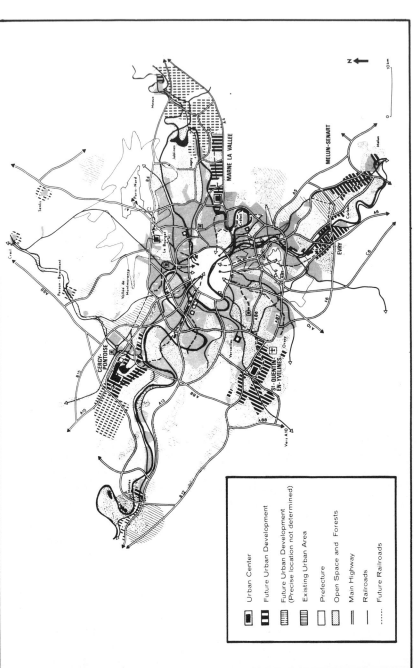

Figure 1–2. The revised Paris region master plan of 1969. The 1969 revision of the 1965 master plan eliminated three of the eight proposed new towns. Two at Trappes were combined into one, now known as Saint-Quentin-en-Yvelines. Mantes and Beauchamp were eliminated after intense local opposition to the plan. (Préfecture de la Région Parisienne, *La Région parisienne: quatre années d'aménagement et d'équipement* (Paris: Institut d'Aménagement et d'Urbanisme de la Région

Maryland; Greenhills, Ohio; and Greendale, Wisconsin. The projects, built by WPA workers, housed low-income government employees but contained few job opportunities. They suffered from bureaucratic indifference after the first few years of operation. An attempt to build a fourth new town in New Jersey was stopped by a court suit, which eventually resulted in a ruling that the Resettlement Administration was unconstitutional. Administration of the Greenbelt towns passed from one unsympathetic agency to another, ending with the Public Housing Administration. In 1949 the projects were sold. Despite the problems of the Greenbelt towns they made an important contribution to the development of American policy; they demonstrated that with the leadership of the federal government, environmentally attractive, low-income housing projects could be built in the suburbs.[2]

Other than the Greenbelt towns, American new towns have been initiated by private developers, most recently in the 1950s and early 1960s. There are hundreds of communities calling themselves new towns in America today, although most are merely large-scale dormitory suburbs. Induced by the apparent success of many privately sponsored new towns at the time, Congress adopted a national urban growth policy in 1970, in which new towns would play a role. Title VII of the Housing and Urban Development Act of 1970 called for the implementation of a national urban growth policy in the United States, based on a number of urban and regional planning principles. Congress declared that the national urban growth policy should help reduce economic and social disparities among regions and within urban areas through comprehensive treatment of the relationships of poverty, employment, and the growth or decline of urban and rural areas. The president was required to submit a national urban growth policy statement every two years.[3] The bulk of the HUD Act provided government support for the construction of new towns. New towns were cited as an efficient mechanism for the implementation of the social, physical, and economic goals of the national urban growth policy.

Four types of financial assistance were made available under the act:

1. Loan guarantees. Private developers could receive up to $50 million in government guarantees for loans to acquire and develop the new town site. The guarantee could cover up to 80 percent of the land acquisition costs and 90 percent of the land development costs

---

[2]See Joseph L. Arnold, *The New Deal in the Suburbs: A History of the Greenbelt Town Program, 1935–54* (Columbus: Ohio State University Press, 1971).

[3]Public Law 91–609, 84 Stat. 1791, 42 U.S.C. 4501.

incurred by the private developer. A state agency could receive 100 percent of these costs. Thirteen projects received $348 million in commitments, with $299 million actually issued. Two other projects developed by the New York State Urban Development Corporation were given certificates of eligibility for all types of financial assistance other than guarantees. (See table 1–1.)

2. Loans. Loans of up to $20 million for fifteen years per project were authorized to assist the developer in making interest payments on the loans. In 1971, $36 million was released by the administration but rescinded shortly thereafter. No further funds have been made available. However, after several projects defaulted, HUD had to

Table 1–1. The Title VII New Towns

| New Town | Location | Loan Guarantees | | Population (1976) | Jobs (1976) |
		Committed	Issued		
New towns where development is continuing under the original developer					
Harbison	8 mi. northwest of Columbia, S.C.	$24m	$24m	2,800	1,500
Maumelle	12 mi. northwest of Little Rock, Ark.	25m	14m	140	45
St. Charles	25 mi. southeast of Washington, D.C.	38m	38m	9,000	250
Shenandoah	35 mi. southwest of Atlanta, Ga.	40m	25m	7	30
Soul City	45 mi. north of Raleigh, N.C.	14m	10m	55	116
The Woodlands	30 mi. north of Houston, Texas	50m	50m	2,500	1,200
New towns where HUD is acquiring the assets and seeking new developers					
Cedar-Riverside	downtown Minneapolis	$24m	$24m	2,800	1,500
Flower Mound	22 mi. northwest of Dallas, Texas	18m	18m	325	25
Jonathan	25 mi. southwest of Minneapolis, Minn.	21m	21m	2,500	1,500
Park Forest South	30 mi. southwest of Chicago, Ill.	30m	30m	5,800	1,800
Riverton	10 mi. south of Rochester, N.Y.	21m	16m	875	12
New towns being phased out					
Gananda	12 mi. east of Rochester, N.Y.	$22m	$22m	0	40
Newfields	7 mi. northwest of Dayton, Ohio	32m	18m	122	50

make interest payments in connection with the loan guarantees it had issued.

3. Supplementary grants. The new towns were eligible for grants under a variety of federal programs. A new town project that received a federal grant could then get a supplemental grant from HUD to assist the local government's contribution when required. Only $25 million was ever appropriated under this section. The federal categorical grant system was replaced in 1974 by the Community Development Block Grant, under which new towns are eligible.

4. Special planning assistance. An extra $5 million (raised to $10 million) was authorized by Congress for the provision of assistance to the developers for planning innovative social, environmental, or technical projects in the new towns. The administration impounded these funds.

Finally, the New Community Development Corporation was to be established to oversee the program. Originally designed to be independent of other federal agencies, it was eventually placed under HUD and renamed the New Communities Administration. The New Community Development Corporation was able to undertake direct construction of demonstration new towns, although no funds have been appropriated to undertake such an effort.

Why has the Title VII program failed? A HUD white paper, prepared in 1976 with the assistance of the Booz-Allen consultant firm, cited two major defects in the program:

a. Policy failures. The new towns program was never implemented within the context of a national urban growth policy. Instead, it was seen as a method of supporting large-scale private developers. The location of the new towns was not based on planning considerations; sites were selected on the basis of response to applications submitted by developers. Although HUD tried to require the private developers to achieve certain social planning objectives, there was no mechanism of control once funds had been granted. Furthermore, other government social programs, even within HUD, were not coordinated with the new towns. Developers who wished to build low-income housing, which requires government financial assistnace, could not secure the funds from HUD.

b. Implementation failures. The method of financial assistance was infeasible. Private developers were forced to borrow large sums of money to pay for land acquisition and site preparation costs. The loan guarantees did not provide sufficient benefit to offset the high risks of the efforts. Even with the guarantees, the developers still had to repay their loans. The interest payments alone turned out to be more than the revenue that could be generated from land sales in the early

years of the projects. The federal support could not salvage projects
that were basically poor financial risks. The recession of 1973–74
sealed the doom of many Title VII developers who could not generate
a market for their land.[4]

In January 1975, HUD placed a moratorium on any further Title VII
project applications. The following year, it reevaluated the thirteen
original projects. Six projects were permitted to continue with
refinancing for the original developer, while the assets of the other
seven were acquired by HUD. A new developer is being sought for
five of the new towns, while the other two — Gananda, near Rochester,
N.Y., and Newfields, near Dayton, Ohio — were terminated.

In contrast to the situation in the United States new towns have
been built in Great Britain and France within the context of national
urban growth policies. Although the precise planning policies and the
role of new towns differ in the two countries, there are strong
similarities.

The British new towns policy was initiated after World War II, a
part of a comprehensive planning system developed by the newly
elected Labor government, almost precisely fifty years after the
publication of Ebenezer Howard's book. Howard was not content
simply to expound his idea in a book; he wanted to generate interest
in the actual construction of garden cities. He secured enough
support to start construction of the First Garden City at Letchworth in
1903, with a second begun at Welwyn in 1920. His followers
organized the Garden Cities Association, now the Town and Country
Planning Association, to encourage government and popular support
for national planning and new towns.

Two government reports during the interwar years supported the
principle of constructing new towns in Britain, but the turning point
was the Report of the Royal Commission on the Distribution of the
Industrial Population (known as the Barlow Report) in 1940. The
Barlow Commission was appointed "to inquire into the causes which
have influenced the present geographic distribution of the industrial
population of Great Britain and the probable direction of any change
in that direction in the future; to consider what social, economic or
strategic disadvantages arise from the concentration of industries or
of the industrial population in large towns or in particualr areas of the

[4]U.S. Department of Housing and Urban Development, New Communities Administration, *New Communities: Problems and Potentials,* 5 vols. (Washington, D.C.: New
Communities Administration, 1976).

country; and to report what remedial measures if any should be taken in the national interest."[5]

The industrial distribution was caused by changing technological conditions, such as the substitution of electricity for coal and the end of the transportation monopoly held by railroads. Expanding industries no longer sought locations near sources of raw materials but were concentrating in the largest markets, such as London and Birmingham. Barlow noted the social, economic, and strategic disadvantages of industrial concentration. Although the commission did not specifically recommend the construction of new towns, its argument against continued unchecked growth of the big cities coincided with that of the new towns supporters.

The Barlow Report's recommendations against further concentration in London and other big cities became the basis for postwar planning policies. Sir Patrick Abercrombie was appointed to prepare plans for the London region, as well as the central area.[6] The Greater London Plan of 1944 divided the London region into four rings. The inner ring, which had been severely damaged during the war, was to be comprehensively redeveloped at lower densities. The second ring — the older suburbs — would maintain a stable population level, although some moderation was needed. The third ring was a green belt, where further building would be prohibited and permanent open space safeguarded. Beyond the green belt, growth would be concentrated in new towns, designed to receive the "overspill" of people and activities displaced from the inner ring.

Britain elected a majority Labor government for the first time in 1945, committed to large-scale social and economic planning. The most important urban planning policies included:

1. Nationalization of land rights. All proposed changes in the use of land had to receive the permission of local authorities. Owners prohibited from developing their land could receive financial compensation. Funds for compensation came from a 100 percent "betterment" tax on the increased land values accruing to owners of land with development permission.

2. Statutory plans. Local authorities were required to prepare plans showing where development could take place and areas to be

[5] Royal Commission on the Distribution of the Industrial Population, *Report*, Cmd. 6153 (London: His Majesty's Stationery Office, 1940).

[6] Patrick Abercrombie, *Greater London Plan, 1944* (London: His Majesty's Stationery Office, 1945): and J. H. Forshaw and Patrick Abercrombie, *County of London Plan* (London: His Majesty's Stationery Office, 1943).

protected. Permission to develop land could be given only if it were consistent with the development plan.

3. New towns. A commission was established under the direction of Lord Reith (who had organized the BBC) to prepare strategy for the implementation of a new program.[7] Reith proposed sites for new towns, many of which coincided with Abercrombie's suggestion, as well as the methods of financing and administering the new towns.

Fourteen new towns were designated between 1947–51, including eight outside of London and two in Scotland. These so-called Mark I new towns were primarily planned for intraregional purposes. They were designed to accommodate the overspill from the central areas of London, Birmingham, Liverpool, and Glasgow, that is, the families needing homes as a result of the planned reduction in the number of dwellings in the redeveloped central areas. When the Conservative party regained power in 1951 they permitted work to continue on the new towns but designated only one additional new town between 1951–63. In the early 1960s, however, the Conservatives initiated a second wave of new towns, primarily to meet interregional needs. Thus the usefulness of new towns has now been accepted by both political parties. Thirty-three new towns have been designated in Britain, containing two million people and one million jobs.

Is there a role for new towns in the United States? Despite the problems of the Title VII new towns, HUD thinks so. Although the nation's population is increasing less rapidly now than in the past, large-scale redistribution of that population continues. People and jobs are still moving from central cities to suburbs, and from the north and east to the south and west. In the absence of effective planning, the suburbs and newer cities of the south and west are organized in a wasteful, costly, and environmentally damaging pattern of sprawl while the central cities of the northeast try to meet the needs of an increasingly poor and nonwhite population with the dwindling tax base. Like other countries, the United States has both intraregional and interregional problems that call for a coordinated planning response. According to a 1976 HUD white paper, "The nation's experience with new town development, both private and public, indicate that new towns, properly located, designed, financed, managed and supported, represent a cost-efficient, environmentally-sound, socially-desirable, and consumer-attractive tool for intelligent growth management."[8]

---

[7]New Towns Committee, *Interim Report*, Cmd. 6759; *Second Interim Report*, Cmd. 6794; *Final Report*, Cmd. 6876 (London: His Majesty's Stationery Office, 1946).

[8]U.S. Dept. of HUD, New Communities Administration, *New Communities* p.99.

How can the United states revive its new towns program? Many of the difficulties associated with the development of a new towns program in the United States are due to an attempt to emulate the administrative and financial procedures adopted in Britain. As the HUD white paper relates, "While French and Scandinavian new town programs helped to inspire interest in the development of an American counterpart, the British program most influenced Title VII's design."[9] The central argument of this book is that many of the problems faced by the French planners in the implementation of their new towns are comparable to those now experienced by the United States. The French experience deserves the careful attention of American policy makers, because if the French could overcome the obstacles to the development of new towns there, so could the Americans.

DEVELOPMENT OF THE NEW TOWNS IDEA IN FRANCE

In certain ways the French new towns represent a departure from the traditional concept of new towns, as developed primarily in Great Britain. The French new towns are large projects, ranging in size from 140,000 to 500,000 residents. They are not separated from the rest of the built-up area by green belts. Because of different tastes in urban design the French new towns contain more high-rise apartments than almost anywhere in the world. The French new towns could in fact be called "new downtowns" in view of the importance being placed on development of large town centers.

However, despite the differences in architectural execution the French new towns share the same functional rationale with other new towns projects around the world. The French new towns, like their counterparts elsewhere, are designed to organize large-scale urban growth in an orderly manner, with an efficient provision of required services and facilities, while at the same time achieving a socially balanced community.

The sixth national plan provided the official government statement of the purposes of the French new towns policy. According to the sixth plan, the new towns are designed to accomplish four primary goals:

1. to restructure the suburbs by organizing new concentrations of employment, housing, and services;

2. to reduce the amount of commuting and ease the transport problems in particular urban regions;

[9]Ibid. p. 10.

3. to create truly self-contained cities, as measured by a balance between jobs and housing, a variety of different jobs and housing, the provision of housing and supporting services at the same time and place, the rapid creation of urban centers, and concern for recreational facilities and environmental protection;

4. to serve as laboratories for experiments in urban planning and design. [10]

Although the sixth plan differs somewhat in terms of organizing the rationale for new towns in France, the basic twofold pattern, which runs throughout the new town literature, is clearly observed. The French new towns have distinctive visual characteristics, but the underlying functions of the policy—to concentrate regional growth in an efficient manner and to create socially balanced communities— have been maintained.

In order to understand why French planners support the construction of new towns it is necessary to examine the relationship between the new towns and other planning policies in France. Like other European countries, France initiated national planning policies after World War II. In contrast to the British, who started the construction of new towns soon after the war, French planners had other planning priorities. New towns have been developed in France only in a second generation of postwar planning in the 1960s.

French planning since World War II has been characterized by two major principles, the stimulation of national economic growth and the reduction of regional disparities. The rationale for these two planning goals may be examined in more detail.

Economic planning

Although France, like the rest of Europe, required large-scale reconstruction of its industrial base because of wartime destruction, it had a more fundamental economic problem. For nearly a century, between 1850–1950, while the rest of the western world rapidly expanded, France had been relatively stagnant economically and had not increased in population.

Until 1850, the growth of the French economy and population had not differed dramatically from that of other countries. France had the largest population in Europe except for Russia. It had been the second country (after Britain) to begin the process of industrial modernization in the eighteenth century. Although the new industrial

[10]France, Office of the Prime Minister, *Programme finalisé des villes nouvelles* (Paris: Ministère de l'Equipment et du Logement, 1971).

system spread much more slowly across France than elsewere, nonetheless France appeared to have established a strong, balanced foundation for long-term economic prosperity. However, France stopped growing after 1850. The population, which had grown from 27 million in 1800 to 38 million in 1865, stagnated for the next eighty years. In 1946 the population was 40.5 million, an increase of only 2.5 million in eighty years, an average annual rate of increase of less than 0.1 percent. The lack of growth was due to the abnormally low birth rates in France, rather than to unusually high mortality rates.[11] By the end of World War II England, Germany, and Italy, as well as the Soviet Union, were all more populous than France.

During this 100-year period the French economy expanded far more slowly than the rival European states. Diffusion of technological innovations to rural areas was much slower. National monetary policies did not support speculative economic ventures. Few risks were taken by French businessmen. Most of the industrial inventions were imported to France by foreigners. Isolated experiments and innovations sprang up in France, but they were not developed or accepted throughout the economy.[12]

In response to the long-term economic problems, as well as the wartime destruction, France established an economic planning program after World War II. Supported in part by Marshall Plan funds, France established its first national plan in 1947, under the direction of Jean Monnet. The plan set priorities in national investment for the purpose of stimulating recovery and long-term growth. Public funds were channeled into six industries considered most critical to the national economy: coal, electricity, steel, cement, agricultural machinery, and transportation. Some key sectors were nationalized in whole or in part.[13]

The process of creating national plans has been institutionalized in France. These plans now routinely set national investment priorities for five-year periods. In 1976 the French completed the sixth five-year plan and began the seventh. The plans have reflected the nation's predominant economic concerns, such as industrial expansion, unemployment, inflation, social services, relations to the Common

[11]The cause of the unusually low birth rate has been inconclusively debated. Explanations include the lack of economic growth, the inheritance laws, and the sophistication of French civilization. See Joseph Spengler, *France Faces Depopulation* (Durham: Duke University Press, 1938).

[12]See Claude Fohlen, "The Industrial Revolution in France," in *Essays in French Economic History*, ed. Rondo Cameron (Homewood, Ill.: Richard D. Irwin, Inc., 1970).

[13]See Stephen Cohen, *Modern Capitalist Planning: The French Model* (London: Weidenfeld and Nicolson, 1969).

Market, etc. The plan has become a forum for political debates over the relative merits of alternative economic policies. As was indicated earlier, the sixth plan included the new towns among the national investment priorities.

The national plan is prepared by a government organization called the Commissiariat Générale du Plan (CGP), or National Planning Commission.The CGP was designed to complement rather than compete with the established ministries, such as the ministry of national economy and finance or the ministry of equipment. It has a relatively small staff (about sixty) but is attached directly to the prime minister's office. The CGP relies on the various ministries to conduct research and implement the plan. Its role is to coordinate goals and priorities established by the various factions in the government.

Regional planning

The overall economic and demographic stagnation in France during the nineteenth century and the first half of the twentieth century masks the sharp patterns of redistribution going on. As in other countries, French cities were growing faster than the rural areas, but the trends were more dramatic.

Until the middle of the nineteenth century, economic and demographic growth was rather evenly distributed around France. Cities expanded but so did the countryside. Economic expansion was achieved without a massive migration to the cities. Industries such as textiles operated efficiently with rural home-based labor, rather than in costly factories in big cities. Although Paris had long ago been established as the most important city in France, the regional centers such as Lille, Lyon, and Marseille shared in the national growth.

After 1850 the pattern of balanced national growth was destroyed. People and jobs were increasingly concentrated in the Paris region, which started to grow at the expense of the rest of the country. From 1801–51 Paris grew by around 500,000 people and France as a whole by 9 million. After the 1866 census the rural areas began to lose population rapidly while urban growth was increasingly concentrated in Paris. From a city of one million in 1851, Paris grew to 1.8 million in 1866, 2.5 million in 1891, and 6.6 million in 1946. Between 1866 and 1946, the Paris region increased by 4.8 million people, while France as a whole increased by only 2.5 million. France outside Paris therefore actually declined by 2.3 million people during this eighty-year period. Paris increased its share of the national population from two percent in 1800 and five percent in 1866 to fifteen percent by 1946.

In contrast to the situation in England, where governments since the time of Elizabeth I had tried to stop the growth of London, the French encouraged the growth of their capital city. Paris competed with Berlin, Rome, and Vienna to become the largest and most important city on the continent. Public works projects were concentrated in the Paris region. Virtually all roads and railroads converged there. Baron Haussmann, prefect of the Department of the Seine from 1853–71 under Napoleon III, directed a massive building effort in Paris. Wide boulevards and large squares were carved out of densely packed neighborhoods. Large parks were developed on the fringe of the built-up area, including the Bois de Boulogne, the Bois de Vincennes, Buttes Chaumont, Montsouris, and Parc Monçeau. The water and sewer system of Paris were modernized (and are the tourist attractions today). The facilities built by Haussmann proved sufficient to accommodate the demands for public services until well into the twentieth century. Since Haussmann's day, Paris has also developed an extensive subway system.

The concentration of physical development in Paris was complemented by administrative centralization in such areas as government and banking. Applications for loans by individuals or industries in the provinces took much longer to process than identical loans applied for in Paris, because provincial bank branches had to send the request to the central office in Paris for approval. Government decision making was increasingly centralized. The most famous anecdote was that the minister of education in Paris could tell a visitor exactly what line of Vergil was being recited at that moment in every classroom in France.[14] Paris became increasingly dominant as the cultural and intellectual center of France. Investment in theaters, museums, and universities was concentrated there. Per capita income in Paris was twice as high as the poorest parts of France.

After World War II, the French public became increasingly aware of the growing imbalance between Paris and the rest of the country. The most important contribution to this awareness was the publication of a book called *Paris and the French Desert*, written by a geographer, J. -F. Gravier. Gravier brought to public attention the role of government policies in concentrating national growth in Paris. He warned that if existing policy continued, France outside of Paris would be a cultural and economic wasteland.[15]

[14]Michel Crozier, *The Bureaucratic Phenomenon* (Chicago: The University of Chicago Press, 1964), p. 239.

[15]J. -F. Gravier, *Paris es le désert français* (Paris: Flammarion, 1947).

Since World War II the French government has attempted to reverse the trend of concentrating resources in Paris. At the same time that the national plans were being developed by the CGP, the ministry of construction — the agency then responsible for much of the government investment in public works projects — took the lead in the development of regional redistribution policies. Programs were formulated to divert growth from the Paris region to the rest of France through a system of permits and financial incentives.

The agency responsible for implementing regional development policies within the ministry of construction was the Département d'Aménagement du Territoire (DAT). During the 1950s DAT was criticized for its failure to discriminate among different industries. By urging all industries to locate in less developed areas, the DAT failed to take into account the different impacts that different industries have on particular regions. The DAT approach to regional development was called "saupoudrage," or powdering. Critics claimed that sustained growth in the less-developed regions could only be fostered if certain key industries were directed there. The DAT was also handicapped by the fact that the disbursement of financial incentives was controlled by the minister of finance, who had other priorities besides regional development.[16]

By the early 1960s the division of responsibilities in the government between economic planning and regional development had become absurd. The DAT planners within the ministry of construction were engaged in the preparation of a national physical plan for the location of new equipment at the same time the CGP was engaged in the preparation of the fourth national plan for economic priorities. It was clear that the regional development policies of the ministry of construction were increasingly intertwined with the national economic planning process. Coherent integration of the two efforts was needed.

Beginning with the fourth national plan (1962–65), the CGP was required to examine the regional impact of all investment proposals. Previously, the national plans divided the study of the economy into different sectors. Today the national plans break down the goals and targets by regions as well as by sectors of the economy. The national plan therefore is a matrix of targets for particular sectors and particular regions. For example, the plan sets a goal for overall housing starts in France but also distributes that total among the regions.

New organizations were created at the regional level to assist the central administration with the establishment of regional economic

[16]George Ross and Stephen Cohen, *The Politics of French Regional Planning* (Baltimore: The Johns Hopkins University Center for Metropolitan Planning and Research, 1973).

policies. France was divided into twenty-one regions, each headed by a regional or "superprefect" (fig. 1–3). The regional prefect consults an advisory commission (the Commission de Développement Economique Régional, or CODER), which contains between twenty and fifty labor and business leaders, local politicians, and other prominent individuals. Each region is given a share of the national plan, called the "tranche régionale," or regional slice. Each of the twenty-one regional prefects, with the advice of CODER, establishes priorities within the region. The regional prefect has considerable discretion in allocating resources to specific projects within the region, such as housing, secondary roads, and schools. However the region cannot, for example, use housing funds for roads. Projects of national importance, such as universities, airports, and expressways, are excluded from the regional prefect's concern.

While the CGP retained responsibility for the development of the national plans, a new national agency was created to ensure that actual investment patterns within the various ministries followed the overall regional development priorities established in the plan. This organization is the Délégation à l'Aménagement du Territoire et à l'Action Régionale (DATAR), the delegation for regional planning. It works with the established ministries so that the investment program of each ministry is consistent with national goals for regional development. Like the CGP, the DATAR works with the existing bureaucracy but answers directly to the prime minister. The DATAR can not command the traditional ministries to adhere to established regional policies, but its close relationship with the prime minister enhances its influence.[17] Its principal power is the right to review the annual budgets prepared by the various ministries. All proposed projects are examined by the DATAR to determine if they are consistent with regional policies. If the DATAR opposes the plans of a traditional ministry, the conflict is settled by the prime minister.

---

[17]According to Ross and Cohen,

The DATAR, modeled after the Planning Commission, was deliberately designed not to pose a direct threat to existing ministries. The fact that it was too small in staff and resources and too weak in legal powers to act on its own constituted a fundamental guarantee to the ministries: like the Plan, it cannot replace them; it cannot command them. DATAR cannot become a super-ministry. It must work within the existing structure of bureaucratic competence and power, trying to initiate and coordinate action by other ministries. But unlike the Plan, which developed during a period of weak, unstable governments and strong, independent bureaucracies, and consequently stressed political non-commitment and independence, DATAR was created in a period of strong Gaullist governments. It has been much closer to purely political undertakings than was the Plan in its early days. Though headed by a 'Minister,' DATAR is not an independent ministry. It was attached directly to the Prime

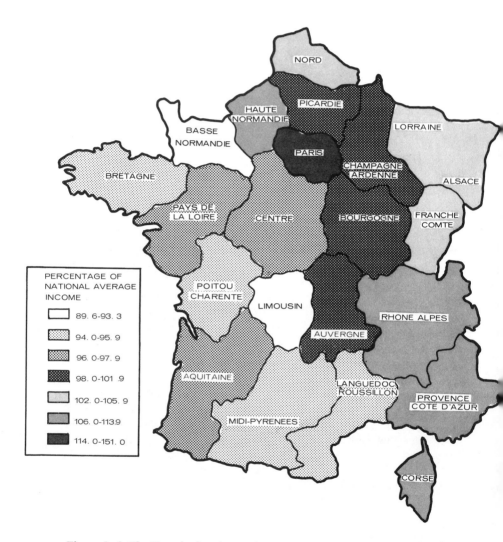

Figure 1–3. The French planning regions. The map indicated the variation in per capita income by regions in 1970. Despite the narrowing of the gap since World War II, the Paris region has nearly a fifty percent higher per capita income than any other region in France and nearly twice the per capita income of the poorest regions.

Minister's Office. But DATAR's attachment has been more intimate in political terms. Among its other consequences, this close political attachment has been an important source of its influence in dealing with other administrations. (Ibid., pp. 19-20.)

The DATAR can also directly finance projects through a small fund that it manages. This fund is called the Fonds d'Intervention pour l'Aménagement du Territoire (FIAT), the fund for regional planning assistance. One of the largest projects supported by the DATAR is the development of Languedoc-Roussillon as a tourist region. Originally a primitive swamp-infested region on the Mediterranean between Marseille and the Spanish border, Languedoc is now being prepared for tourism. Included in the effort is the development of several new communities, with hotels and other tourist needs. New infrastructure is needed throughout the region to support a large population. Many of the administrative and financing techniques first attempted in Languedoc were later applied to the new towns program, although the French government does not consider the Languedoc projects themselves to be new towns.

The DATAR has been responsible for the development of a rather sophisticated regional development policy in France, still based on opposition to further demographic and economic growth of Paris. In contrast to the earlier situation, relatively strong tools are now available to implement this policy. Growth is discouraged in Paris and encouraged elsewhere by a number of measures.

All new housing units or firms above a certain size must obtain a permit to locate anywhere in France. The DATAR has limited the number of new dwellings and offices that can be established in the Paris region. At the moment, growth there is held to around 100,000 dwelling units and 700,000 square meters of office space per year. A firm seeking a permit to be in Paris must demonstrate that no other location in France is feasible. Even in that case the DATAR will strongly encourage the firm to select a suburban location, such as a new town, rather than central Paris. Permits for construction elsewhere in France are granted much more readily.

Regional development policies are also implemented through financial incentives. Firms that do receive permits to locate in the Paris region must pay a special charge, depending on the exact location within the region. On the other hand, a variety of subsidies are given firms that locate elsewhere in France. The country is divided into five zones; industries that locate in the poorest areas, such as Brittany, receive the heaviest subsidies, while those in Paris receive none.

The DATAR has concluded that the most effective way to counteract the influence of Paris is to concentrate investment in relatively few locations rather than to spread it uniformly around the provinces. The most pragmatic way to achieve the long-term objective of reducing the domination of Paris is the encouragement of *métropoles d'équilibre,* or growth poles. The rationale of the growth pole theory, as developed by Perroux, Boudeville, and other French regional economists, is that a few industries have much more of an impact on regional growth than the others. The presence in the region of these key, or propulsive, industries will foster the development of other supporting industries nearby. The location of the propulsive industries should be the main concern of regional development strategies. Because there are only a few, they should be located where they will do the most good.[18]

The DATAR selected eight urban regions to serve as focal points for the establishment of propulsive industries: Marseille, Lyon, Lille, Bordeaux, Toulouse, Nantes-St. Nazaire, Strasbourg, and Nancy-Metz, all large urban areas. They were chosen with the reasoning that the strong pull of Paris could be counteracted only by other large cities. Unlike the rural areas or small towns, the *métropoles d'équilibre* were already large enough to offer supporting services and facilities to meet the initial needs of propulsive industries.

PLANNING FOR THE PARIS REGION

While national attention was focused on correcting the historical imbalances between Paris and the provinces, the Paris region continued to grow, from 6.6 million people in 1946 to 8.4 million by 1962. The nineteenth-century roads, parks, and sewers that had served Paris for many years were no longer adequate. Much of the housing in Paris was overcrowded and lacking modern sanitary conveniences. The housing shortage was severe, because of the years of low construction rates, wartime damage, and the large population increase. Effective planning was stymied by the absence of strong local authorities, inappropriate programs, and hostility on the part of the national planners toward the continued growth of the Paris region. In the absence of strong planning controls the Paris region rapidly expanded during the 1940s and 1950s in a sprawling, undisciplined fashion, aggravating social problems.

The Paris region has become more and more spatially divided into socially segregated units. The basic problem is that more people wish to located their homes and activities in the city center than the space allows, given current building techniques and the need for historical preservation. This pressure to locate in Paris drives out space-intensive activities in favor of those requiring little space, and attracts

---

[18] See Jacques Boudeville, *Problems of Regional Economic Planning* (Edinburgh: Edinburgh University Press, 1966), and Niles Hansen, *French Regional Planning* (Bloomington: Indiana University Press, 1968).

those who are most willing to pay for the location. Thus, offices are expanding in the center while factories move out, and the well-to-do stay in the center while the poor are priced out. Concentration of attention on the center of the city has brought a neglect of the surrounding suburban areas, where the activities and people unable to remain in the center are relocated.

The Paris region has also been spatially segregated between the east and west. The population is divided about evenly between east and west, but two-thirds of the jobs are in the west. During the 1960s one-third of the new population, three-fourths of the employment, and four-fifths of the offices were located in the west.

Paris has always played a dominant role in the nation's economic affairs. The same pressures that worked for concentration of businesses in Paris also produced competition for space in the center itself. In the older parts of Paris classes were traditionally sorted out vertically as well as horizontally. Wealthier families tended to live on the second or third floors, just above the street level and storefronts. The poorest people would live in the basements or lofts, with the worst ventilation. Consequently, everyone enjoyed relatively good accessibility to the opportunities and attractions of central Paris.

Since World War II, the traditional method of accommodating everyone who wanted to be in central Paris has been inadequate. The older buildings require substantial rehabilitation or replacement, after which rents must invariably be raised. Rent controls were applied but have served mainly to postpone inevitably needed work. The rapid rise in housing costs in central Paris today is thus partially the result of many years of frozen prices. With modern building techniques, the lofts of the poor have been turned into fashionable apartments for the wealthy. Working-class neighborhoods are being "rehabilitated" into more expensive, "trendy" boutique districts. Other areas are demolished to make way for luxury high rises.

The intense competition for space in central Paris has priced the poor out of the market. They must live in peripheral projects that have all of the negative features of suburban living and none of the positive. Shopping and recreational facilities are inadequate in the suburbs. Jobs are far away, requiring long-distance commuting on frequently inadequate public transportation systems. Most of the social problems are found in these suburban areas.[19]

Strong pressures for a central location are also expressed by firms seeking office space. This phenomenon is not limited to Paris, of course. Competition for space is unusually intense in central Paris,

[19] See Jean Lojkine, *La Politique urbain dans la région parisienne, 1945–1972* (Paris: Mouton, 1976).

though, for two reasons. Attempts by the national planners to reduce the dominance of Paris have limited the number of new office buildings constructed. In addition, the historical importance and beauty of central Paris severely constrains the amount of possible new construction. Although a few high-rise offices have been permitted in central Paris, their clearly perceived glaring incompatibility with the historic city makes it increasingly difficult for further high rises to be built. Therefore, offices must be squeezed into older, low-rise structures. As in other cities, factories and warehouses, the source of many "working-class" jobs, are moving out of central Paris to the suburbs because they need room to expand. Employment growth in central Paris is due entirely to the expansion of offices.

Central Paris, with about one-fourth of the region's population in 1968, had one-third of the secondary (manufacturing) jobs and over one-half of the tertiary (office) jobs. The inner suburbs contained around 40 percent of the population and the same percentage of the region's secondary jobs, but only one-fourth of the tertiary. The four outer departments of the Paris region, with 30 percent of the population, contained only one-fifth of the secondary and tertiary jobs. The distribution of secondary jobs matches the distribution of population to a large degree, but the office sector—the sector absorbing virtually all of the increase in jobs—is concentrated in central Paris (table 1–2).

Table 1–2. Distribution of Residents and Jobs in the Paris Region

Location	Population	Jobs	Offices
Central Paris	25.8%	47.1%	68.2%
Inner suburbs	41.5	30.0	26.7
Outer suburbs	32.9	22.9	5.1

NOTE: The inner suburbs are defined as the departments of Seine–Saint-Denis, Val-de-Marne, and Hauts de Seine. The outer suburbs are defined as the departments of Essonne, Seine-et-Marne, Val-d'Oise, and Yvelines, Cergy-Pontoise new town is in the department of Val-d'Oise. Evry is in Essonne. Marne-la-Vallée is within three departments: Seine–Saint-Denis, Val-de-Marne, and Seine-et-Marne. Melun-Sénart is in Seine-et-Marne. Saint-Quentin is in Yvelines.

Planning policies in the Paris region prior to the formulation of the new towns idea have aggravated these existing imbalances. Housing programs were designed to alleviate the severe shortage following World War II. Large-scale housing estates, called "*grands ensembles*," were planned in the suburbs during the 1950s and 1960s. Today around one million people live in these *grand ensembles* outside of Paris, about one-third of the population of the outer suburbs. Nearly one-half of the population increase of the Paris region since 1954 has been concentrated in *grand ensembles* (fig. 1–4).[20]

The *grands ensembles* are considered by most French planners today to be unsatisfactory living environments. A relatively high degree of crime and other social pathologies has been observed in them. The planners blame the high incidence of social problems on the lack of social and physical diversity in the projects. Because the purpose of the *grands ensembles* was to provide a large quantitiy of housing, the projects generally consist of several high-density apartment towers. Shopping and recreation facilities near the projects are usually inadequate, and employment opportunities are rare. Residents are required to commute long distances to work in central Paris or in other suburbs. One study has shown that 20 percent of the workers in one large project spend more than one hour to reach work. Commuting was aggravated by the relatively poor public transportation in the suburbs.

The social composition of the residents of these *grand ensembles* also reflects a lack of diversity. The age distribution of the residents shows a preponderance of children under ten and adults between twenty-five and forty, with almost a complete absence of individuals in their early twenties or over fifty. The apartment units have mainly three and four rooms, suitable for families with one or two children but not for individuals or large families. The income distribution is similarly narrow, with most workers performing routine office functions.

The most important planning program affecting the distribution of jobs in the Paris region has been the construction of La Défense. Like the *grands ensembles*, La Défense has exacerbated the social problems of the Paris region. It is a large-scale office complex located in the western suburbs. In response to the pressures for additional office space in the Paris region, the government approved a plan in 1958 to redevelop a large district west of the central area. The most important axis in Paris, which extends west from the Louvre through the Tuileries, Concorde, Champs-Elysées, Arc de Triomphe, and Neuilly, now terminates at the modern high rises of La Défense. The first stage of the operation, on 130 hectares, will be completed shortly; the project contains around 1.5 million square meters of offices, 300,000 square meters of commercial space, and 100,000

---

[20]See Paul Clerc, *Les Grands Ensembles banlieues nouvelles* (Paris: Presses Universitaires de France, 1967); Jean Duquesne, *Vivre à Sarcelles? Le Grand Ensemble et ses problèmes* (Paris: Editions Cujas, 1966); and Merlin, *Villes nouvelles.*

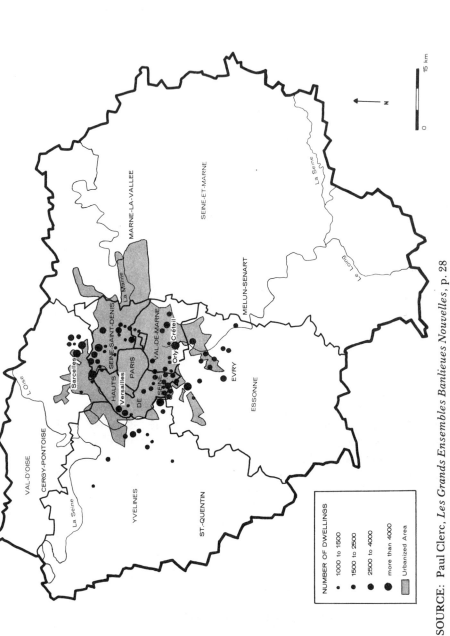

SOURCE: Paul Clerc, *Les Grands Ensembles Banlieues Nouvelles*, p. 28

Figure 1–4. *Grands ensembles* in the Paris region. The map shows the *grands ensembles* of more than 1,000 dwellings. Although located closer to central Paris than the new towns, the *grands ensembles* suffer from poorer transportation links and fewer services within the project areas. Most consist entirely of high-rise apartment towers.

jobs. Future extensions are now being planned. Around thirty percent of the new offices being built in the entire Paris region are now concentrated in La Défense. The result of this concentration in La Défense is a strengthening of the patterns of spatial segregation in the Paris region, for the project represents an extension of the regional office center along a western axis, rather than a fundamental reorientation of the direction of growth, to spread offices more evenly throughout the region.[21]

A master plan was created for the Paris region but was already outdated when published in 1960. This plan, called the PADOG, called for a limit to the growth of the Paris region. A tight line was drawn around the region, surrounded by a green belt in which no new projects were to be located. All growth would be concentrated within the continuously built-up area. By 1960, both the physical boundaries and population projections of the PADOG had been exceeded in the Paris region.[22]

Responding to the need for coherent planning policies in the Paris region, President de Gaulle asked his old friend Paul Delouvrier to see what he could do about the situation. The president appointed Delouvrier as the first head of a new Paris regional government. A strong, dominant personality, Delouvrier is considered the father of French new towns. He is universally cited as the first French planning official to advocate the development of new towns and actively to work for their realization. He was able to use his strength and influence, especially with the president and the minister of finance, to transform the vision of new towns into concrete reality.

In the early 1960s Delouvrier sent his planners around the world to examine planning policies in other cities. French officials at that time seemed to suffer a temporary loss of self-confidence. The traditional French attitude of hostility to foreign ideas was replaced by an aggressive desire to plan Paris with the best tools available from the rest of the world. The new towns policies in Britain, Scandinavia, and Eastern Europe were judged successful by the French.[23]

[21]The head of La Défense development corporation, Jean Millier, was formerly working with the new town studies. He has claimed that La Défense is not really in competition with the new towns. Given the proximity to central Paris and the price advantages, office firms are flocking to La Défense, while the new towns must scramble to get such firms. (Interview, July 1974).

[22]France, Ministère de la Construction, *Plan d'Aménagement et d'Organisation générale de la région parisienne* (Paris: Ministère de la Construction, 1961). For a description of the PADOG plan, see Peter Hall, *The World Cities* (New York: World University Library, 1966).

[23]See for example, Institut d'Aménagement et d'Urbanisme de la Région Parisienne, *Cahiers de l'Institut d'Aménagement et d'Urbanisme de la Région Parisienne* (Paris: Institut d'Aménagement et d'Urbanisme de la Région Parisienne, 1967), vols. 8, 9; and Merlin, *Villes nouvelles.*

Delouvrier's rationale for advocating the construction of new towns outside of Paris was based on the demographic "realities" as he saw them. First of all, it was clear that the geographic area of urbanization must expand, for even if the population were to remain static in the region, each inhabitant would demand more space for housing, services, and equipment, such as cars. However, the population was not going to remain static; even if migration from the provinces were halted, the population would still rise because of the larger number of births than deaths. From 8.4 million people in 1962, Paris would "realistically" grow to 14 million by 2000.

Given the need to expand the surface of the Paris region, the choice is between continuous development and isolated points of growth. The latter was considered infeasible, according to Delouvrier, because "it requires a sharper discipline or control than the French people would accept." The alternative of continuous development normally implies sprawl, or, as the French call it, "tache d'huile" (oil slick), a pattern considered equally unacceptable. The desirable pattern would be to promote continuous growth, not in all directions but along selected axes or corridors, with the other axes retained as open space. New towns are desirable as focal points within the axes of development in order to provide the services and entertainment otherwise found only in the center of Paris.[24]

Although the rationale for constructing the provincial new towns is not entirely contradictory to that for the Paris new towns, it is clear that the two are not fully compatible. The Paris new towns are designed to organize the "inevitable" growth of that region in an efficient manner. The provincial new towns are designed to organize the nationally beneficial growth outside of Paris in an efficient manner.

Despite the fact that four of the nine French new towns are being built in the provinces, the program is still perceived in France as essentially Paris-oriented, because the strongest supporters of new towns have been in the Paris regional government. To the DATAR, the Paris new towns represented a counterinfluence to their policy of discouraging growth in the Paris region. Why then did the DATAR support new towns? To some extent, the DATAR's support for new towns was a result of Delouvrier's pressure. Delouvrier, aware that national support could not be expected for Paris new towns alone, urged the national planners to consider new towns in the provinces.

---

[24]Interview with Paul Delouvrier, July 1974, my translation.

Whether the DATAR would have proposed the provincial new towns without Delouvrier's strong urgings is unknown; but it is certainly true that support for the Paris new towns represents an exception to the national planners' opposition to new large-scale investments in the Paris region. The reduction in the scope of the Paris new towns program was certainly due in part to the need to balance the sizes of the Paris and provincial new towns efforts.

The two sets of new towns have proceeded simultaneously within a unified national structure of administration and financing. In practice, relatively little competition has developed among the various new towns despite the sharply different origins of the provincial and Paris programs. The most important reason for the lack of conflict over priorities among the various new towns is the overall demographic situation in France. Since the end of World War II long-term demographic trends have been reversed.

Since 1945 the Paris region has continued to grow, from 6.6 million to around 10 million in 1975. However, the Paris region is no longer growing at the expense of the rest of the country. In the three decades since World War II, the French population has grown at a rate of 1 percent per year, after a century of averaging under 0.1 percent per year. This reversal is even more dramatic when compared to other western countries, which have moved closer to zero growth. From the slowest growing country in Europe, France has become one of the fastest. About 20 percent of the increase during this period has been due to migration from former colonies in Africa and Asia, but the rest is attributable to higher birth rates and lower mortality rates.

In 1946 the population of France was some 40.5 million, less than in 1901, and only 2.5 million more than in 1866. Between 1901 and 1946, the Paris region had grown by about two million and the rest of France had lost two million. Since 1946, the Paris region has grown by over three million people, but the nation as a whole has increased by thirteen million. From 40.5 million people in 1946, the population of France increased to 42.5 million in 1954, 46.5 million in 1962, 48.5 million in 1965, and around 53 million by the end of 1975.

As a result of the dynamic demographic situation since World War II, no region of France is growing at the expense of others. The nine new towns do not have to fight very hard among themselves for a piece of the pie because it is a very large pie. Paris is growing but so are the provinces. The new towns, consequently, have little impact on the interregional distribution of growth in France. They are attracting part of the continued growth of the Paris region, and part of the growth of the Lille, Lyon, Marseille, and Rouen regions as well.

2

THE ADMINISTRATIVE
STRUCTURE

When the French planners studied the British new towns
program in the early 1960s the aspect they most admired was the
simple administrative structure. The national government, through
the ministry concerned with urban planning (the Department of the
Environment [DOE] at the moment), makes a determination that a
new town should be built to meet certain needs. The government then
selects the exact site for the project, announces the broad goals for
the particular new town, sets the approximate size and population
targets, and appoints a development corporation to oversee the rest
of the effort. The development corporation is a nonprofit corporation
with most of the powers of a public authority, including the power of
eminent domain over local land owners. The secretary of state for the
environment appoints a board of directors, consisting of politicians,
businessmen, labor leaders, and other prominent citizens. The board
approves the plans and sets general policy. Day-to-day activity is
conducted by a staff of several hundred persons, including planners,
architects, engineers, social workers, economists, and other social
scientists, in addition to various maintenance personnel. The development corporation prepares or oversees the development of the master
plan, which must be approved by the DOE. Once approved, the
corporation carries on virtually all phases of urban development. The
only functions normally not performed by the development corporation
are school construction and provision of routine social services; these
tasks are performed by the local authority. Funds are raised by
fifty-year Treasury loans repaid at a rate of interest comparable to the
prevailing prime rate when the new town was established. National
government control is exercised primarily through the requirements
to submit an annual report and to justify the purpose of each Treasury

loan. In the first new towns built after World War II the development corporation built most of the housing and rented it. With the eventual recovery of the private building industry, recent new towns have included more privately built housing for sale. When construction is virtually completed the development corporation is dissolved and the assets are turned over to the Commission for New Towns for management.

The British administrative structure is considered impractical in the United States for two main reasons: first, local government could not be ignored here even if the federal government decided to undertake direct large-scale urban planning; second, major decisions concerning urban development must be made by the private sector. The French new towns administrative system is recommended for analysis precisely because it deals with these two issues in a manner relevant to American administrative problems. Skeptics in other countries who have argued that government-sponsored new towns are not possible would do well seriously to examine the French experience. Given the administrative problems that had to be overcome in France, if the French could successfully implement a new towns program so could the Americans.

Despite the attractiveness of the simple and effective British administrative structure, the French planners sadly concluded that the system was inapplicable to the realities of French administration. In France, as in the United States, the national government has neither the will nor the power to exclude local authorities and the private sector from the development process. As one French new towns official put it:

> An idea initially advanced by technicians aiming for simplicity and unity of responsibility was to make a clean sweep and set up a single body with jurisdiction over the entire area of the new town and with the responsibility for its construction. Based on early management theory and certain features of the British precedent, this idea was attractive but almost immediately proved unworkable and dangerous. It was unworkable because it upset every precedent and the entire French system of public law, whose administrative and financial rules in practice forbid local authorities to engage "directly" in transactions possessing many of the features coming under private law. It was dangerous because in fact it would cause responsibilities to become confused.[1]

Instead, the French have modified their traditional administrative structure just enough to permit the development of the new towns.

---

[1] J.-E. Roullier, *Administrative and Financial Problems of Creating New Towns in the Paris Area* (Paris: Ministère de l'Aménagement du Territoire, d'Equipement, du Logement, et du Tourisme, 1970), p. 18.

The result is an extremely complex structure involving a number of different agencies, in complete contrast to the simple English system. Although many compromises were required, the new towns are a concrete reality in France.

This chapter will describe the French new towns administrative structure in terms appropriate to American observers. The roles of the different participants will be included, as well as the issues that led the French to select particular mechanisms. One can observe the way in which the different parties required to undertake an urban development scheme are drawn into the new towns process in France. By retaining an important role in the development process the local authorities and private builders are committed to the success of the new towns, although at the price of forcing modifications in the policy outputs of the program.

Three distinct sets of actors can be distinguished in the French new towns development process: (1) the national government whose primary concerns are financing and developing the projects; (2) local authorities, who perform the normal functions of French local govern-ments in the new towns; and (3) private builders and developers, who construct and manage the houses and some nonresidential structures.

The complex new towns administrative structure reflects the almost Byzantine qualities of the French governmental system as a whole. Urban development policy in France is best described as a partnership among the national government, local authorities, and private developers. However, none of the three can be regarded as a homogeneous, unitary group. Within the public sector in particular, a wide variety of conflicting perspectives can be found. In order to understand the new towns administrative structure it is necessary first to examine the members of the partnership. This chapter is concerned with the new towns development process from the public sector view, while chapter four looks at it from the perspective of the private sector.

THE NATIONAL GOVERNMENT ROLE

The French government is characterized by powerful, isolated ministries. Each ministry jealously guards its traditional administra-tive functions and responsibilities from raids by other ministries or new special-purpose organizations. Compared to the United States, ad hoc or interdisciplinary agencies are rare in France. Civil servants respect other ministries' territories in order to avoid retaliatory raids upon themselves. This isolation was reinforced by the traditional system of appointments to the higher civil service and the Grands Corps (the highest level of the civil service).[2] Before 1945 these appointments were made on the basis of competitive examinations administered by each corps or ministry. Therefore, the educational system was designed to prepare students for one particular exam. Because civil servants had studied a very narrow subject, there was little mobility or shared experiences among the services.

This fragmentation among the various ministries has been a major obstacle in the development of coherent rational policies for urban development. The problem is that urban development is not a clear function of one ministry. In actuality three ministries have responsibilities that significantly affect urban policy: the ministries of finance, interior, and equipment. Each is rather strong and relatively free of pressure from other ministries.

The ministry of economic affairs and finance has traditionally been the most powerful ministry in France. It is responsible for preparing the annual budget and for establishing the nation's monetary policies. Funds for most projects that other ministries propose or wish to continue are appropriated by the ministry of finance. It frequently must rank priorities among competing claims of different ministries. Proposed investments in urban development projects are placed in national fiscal perspective by this ministry.

The ministry of finance also controls several financial institutions that make loans and grants for urban development projects. The most important is the Caisse des Dépôts et Consignations (CDC), a

---

[2] The classic study of the French administration is Crozier, *Bureaucratic Phenomenon*. Crozier found a high degree of isolation among workers at all strata in the government. This was produced by the recruitment of different categories of officials from different schools. Virtually no informal relations exist among individuals of different strata; such relations are discouraged because they might produce patterns of favoritism. Instead, all relationships among individuals in different strata are formal. French bureaucrats dislike having to exercise direct face-to-face authority, so that authority is converted to impersonal rules. Conformity and equality within and between strata are achieved by the universal application of impersonal rules, a pattern that heightens the isolation of the individual. Cohesion among officials at all strata is promoted by the universal participation in "*bon plaisir.*" Crozier defines *bon plaisir* as the ability to act arbitrarily at one's own pleasure, a term derived from the concept legitimizing the old monarchy. The authority exercised at one level over the next is absolute in theory, without checks and balances, but must be done in an impersonal way rather than through personal contact. An elaborate system of formal rules has been created to enable officials to exercise *bon plaisir* over lower officials and to rationalize submission to higher ones. Change is difficult because no mechanism exists for instituting reforms except by arbitrary edict from the top strata of civil servants. The French government thus comprises a collection of isolated individuals fiefdoms, each protecting its absolute authority over a narrow range of activities.

national bank established in 1816. It is the largest holder of funds in France, with most assets coming from individual savers who bank in their local post offices. Because of its large size the CDC can regulate the nation's financial market. The ministry of finance, by controlling the CDC, strongly influences the pattern of urban development in many ways. The CDC loans money directly to local authorities and provides the money for a number of other governmental agencies that make grants and loans to local authorities and private developers.

Among the important agencies investing CDC funds in urban development are SCIC, SCET, and FNAFU. SCIC (Société Centrale de la Caisse des Dépôts) is a building company that is directly responsible for the construction of a large amount of housing in France, including many of the *grands ensembles* in the Paris region. SCET helps to finance the construction of other large-scale projects not developed directly by SCIC. Joint public-private companies called the Société d'Economie Mixte (SEM) are established at the local level to undertake comprehensive development.[3] SCET provides part of the funding for these organizations. FNAFU loans money to the local authority or SEM for the installation of roads, sewers, and other infrastructure required in advance of the construction of buildings.

The ministry of finance also controls the Crédit Foncier, or land bank. The Credit Foncier is the largest lender of funds to private developers for housing construction. (The government does not directly build housing in France, with a few exceptions, such as SCIC). The Crédit Foncier provides private developers with mortgage loans, and sometimes with guarantees as well. The amount of the loan or guarantee largely determines the final selling price of the house.

Finally, the finance ministry directs the FDES, a special fund that goes directly to selected projects and agencies, especially the nationalized industries. The investment decisions, set by an interministerial committee, are supposed to be in conformance with the priorities of the national plans.

Prior to World War II the ministry of finance was considered to be very conservative, but in recent years it has become more pragmatic and open to innovative programs of urban development investments.[4] The successful launching of the new towns program is due in large

[3] The SEM was considered an unsatisfactory mechanism for the development of new towns because in French law it could only be created by local authorities, which would have to give up certain development rights and make financial guarantees. The SEM required between thirty-five and fifty percent private sector involvement, which was not yet feasible in the new towns.

[4] Cohen, *Modern Capitalist Planning*, pp. 36–40.

measure to the willingness of the ministry of finance to authorize the required financial assistance.

The minister of interior is the voice of local authorities at the national level. He appoints many local government officials and has ultimate authority over all local actions. The ministry is considered a very traditionalistic organization, opposed to dramatic administrative changes and concerned primarily with preserving the established political power of local authorities. It should be mentioned that a number of local officials are also members of the national assembly. Although some of these officials have been involved in formulating the administrative reforms needed for the development of new towns, most have avoided active support of them.

The Ministère de l'Aménagement du Territoire, d'Equipement, du Logement, et du Tourisme, or ministry of equipment for short, has combined a number of small ministries concerned with various aspects of urban development, as the long name indicates. The equipment ministry is oriented toward encouraging public works projects, such as roads and sewers. It is unequivocably prodevelopment but is divided on the proper location of that growth. The ministry is liberally sprinkled with both supporters and opponents of the new towns program.

The traditional fragmentation and isolation of the ministries has been considerably reduced in recent years. Two major causes for this change include the creation of a strong executive form of government in the Fifth Republic, and the reform of the education system. During the Fourth Republic (1945–58), France had a parliamentary system. Most of the prime ministers were unable to create a strong government because of the fragmentation of political parties in the national assembly. The constitution of the Fifth Republic has delegated most of the power to a president. The president, popularly elected to a seven-year term, appoints the prime minister and cabinet. Charles de Gaulle was president from 1959 to 1969, resigning after reforms he supported were defeated on referendum. Georges Pompidou was elected in 1969 and served until his death in 1974. The former minister of finance, Valéry Giscard d'Estaing, is now president. As all three have been members of conservative parties, the effect has been to foster the coalescence of the various parties into conservative and socialist-oriented coalitions.

The traditional educational system was changed in 1945. Candidates for civil service positions now take one common exam rather than separate exams on narrowly defined subjects. The Ecole Libre des Sciences Politiques, an exclusive private school where most of the higher civil servants had been educated, was nationalized, renamed the Institut d'Etudes Politiques, and made part of the University of

Paris. A new graduate school of administration was established, the Ecole National d'Administration (ENA).

The ENA educational program has emphasized pragmatic decision-making techniques rather than the traditional ideologies. [5] Under the influence of ENA graduates, the French administration now includes interdisciplinary committees and task forces, unheard of prior to the reforms. In the planning field, two recently created examples are the Commissariat Générale du Plan and the DATAR. Many of the current leaders are graduates of ENA, including Giscard and a number of the new towns officials. It is clear that the innovative governmental structures devised for the new towns program were strongly influenced by the ENA pragmatic spirit. The new towns, conceived during the period of Gaullist grandeur, have survived the technocratic age of Giscard because the new towns officials speak the same language as the president.

An interministerial task force was created by the prime minister in 1970 to promote the interests of the new towns within the government. The agency, called the Groupe Central des Villes Nouvelles (GCVN), plays both a technical and policy-making role. It is concerned with gathering data and monitoring the progress of the new towns, particularly in comparison to the goals of the national plans. An especially important function in this regard is the monitoring of the financial status of each new town. A large percentage of the data used in this book was generated or compiled by the GCVN. The GCVN is responsible for ensuring that the investment policies of each ministry are consistent with the overall goals of the French new towns. The annual budget of each ministry are reviewed and rationalized by the GCVN. Proposed expenditures by individual ministries can be changed by the GCVN in order to promote a coherent development program. Furthermore, once the annual budget is established by the GCVN and approved by the cabinet, the national assembly or individual ministries can not make any further cuts. The new towns expenditures appear as a separate line in the annual budgets of each ministry, and this line is immune from cuts.

The GCVN replaced an earlier interministerial working group established in 1966 by the prime minister with representatives of only the ministries of finance, interior, and equipment. The GCVN includes representatives of a dozen ministries, as well as agencies such as the DATAR. Like the rest of the French administrative structure, it is a rather complex organization. Its secretary general plays three roles. First, he is the technical head of a number of research-oriented functions, shown on the right-hand side of figure 2–1. These functions

[5]Ibid., pp. 46–48.

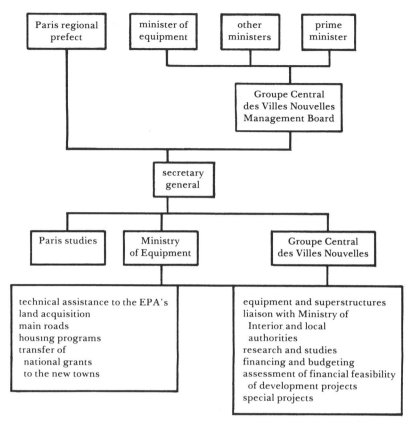

Figure 2–1. Organization of the Groupe des Villes Nouvelles. The GCVN plays three roles. First, it conducts research and studies concerning all aspects of the new towns. Second, it is linked directly to the Ministry of Equipment; in this role the GCVN performs certain functions relating to the provision of new roads, land acquisition, and other infrastructure. Third, the GCVN plays a special role in gathering data about the Paris new towns.

relate primarily to the gathering of statistics and the coordination of the financial studies at each of the nine new towns. About twenty people perform these tasks. The policy-making duties are entrusted to a management board, comprising a president and vice president and representatives of twelve ministries and the departments where new towns are located.

The secretary general of the GCVN is at the same time a representative of the ministry of equipment. He is in charge of the technical and financial assistance that the ministry of equipment has available for the new towns. This arrangement, of course, ensures that the ministry of equipment is strongly committed to new towns. The

GCVN also provides a special service to the Paris regional government by monitoring the progress of the Paris new towns.

THE LOCAL GOVERNMENT PROBLEM

The local government system in France is rather chaotic. France has three tiers of local government, including the twenty-one regional governments recently established. The two traditional levels are the departments and communes. There are ninety-five departments in France, eight of which are in the Paris region. Each is headed by a prefect, appointed by the minister of interior, and by an elected General Council. The prefect of the largest department in the region becomes the regional prefect. Below the departments are the communes, the government closest to the individual citizen. France is divided into some 38,000 communes, with a mean area of 1,428 hectares and a mean population of 1,400. There are 1,305 communes in the Paris region alone. The citizens of each commune elect a mayor and municipal council.

Because the communes are small and have an elected executive, they are considered the guardians of the individual citizen against national government excesses. The department is in reality a branch of the national government. The prefect, appointed by the minister of interior, must play two roles. As the highest official in the department he is naturally concerned with its welfare. As an appointee of the minister of interior, the prefect is also a representative of the national administration, and is authorized to perform state functions at the local level.

Many ministries maintain *missions* of experts in each department. These agencies are a reflection of the traditional administrative centralization in France. Although the *missions* deal with problems of local concern, they are answerable to the national ministries in the Paris offices rather than to local politicians. They also fill a gap in expertise at the local level caused by the inability of local governments to pay for technocrats of their own. The *missions* can be compared to a domestic peace corps. Most decisions concerning priorities for new projects are made by the *missions* from the ministry of equipment, the Direction Départementale d'Equipement (DDE).

Since 1965 France has been divided into twenty-one regional authorities. Each region is headed by a prefect, called a regional or superprefect. The prefect of the largest department in the region is usually appointed regional prefect. The regions are responsible for establishing their own investment priorities consistent with the goals of the national plans. Housing projects with more than 1,000 dwelling units and firms occupying more than 2,000 square meters must receive permits from the region. Regional investment decisions relating to equipment are made by a new organization called the Service Régional d'Equipement (SRE). The SRE, like the DDE, consists of national civil servants assigned to the local government.

A special regional government was created for the Paris region. Until the 1960s the Paris region had contained three departments and 1,305 communes. The departments were considered too large to carry out departmental functions effectively but too small to serve as regional agencies. When Paul Delouvrier was asked by de Gaulle to "do something" about Paris, his first act was to create a regional government. In 1961 the Paris district was created, with Delouvrier appointed the administrative head, called the délégué général. At first the position was primarily advisory. The délégué général was responsible for the development of plans and he could direct local authorities to harmonize their budgets with regard to new equipment. He could propose policies to the government, especially in the transportation field. One of the first priorities set by Delouvrier was the revision of the 1960 PADOG plan for Paris, which was already outdated. He ordered the newly established regional planning agency, the Institut d'Aménagement et d'Urbanisme de la Région Parisienne (IAURP), to develop a more realistic plan. The SDAURP, released in 1965, contained the new towns proposals.

The regional government's powers were strengthened in 1964. The délégué général also became a regional prefect. As in the other twenty-one regions in France, the Paris regional prefect holds considerable discretion over allocating national grants to specific projects. At the same time, the three departments of the Paris region were rearranged into eight new ones. This action required the establishment of five new prefectures (county seats). Two of these five were sited in the new towns of Cergy-Pontoise and Evry. In 1975 a regional assembly was first elected by popular vote. Prior to that time several appointed committees of distinguished citizens advised the regional prefect. The Paris region is now known officially as the Ile-de-France region.

The district has the ability to raise taxes and borrow money. In 1977 districts raised 1.9 billion francs from three main souces. About 50 percent came from a variety of taxes on businesses, about 40 percent from loans, and 10 percent from various user fees and charges. Most of the 1.9 billion francs went for the local share of new transportation projects, including about 50 percent for public transportation and 25 percent for roads; around 14 percent of the highway funds go to projects in the new towns. Twelve percent each went for land

development and construction of various cultural, health, and recreational facilities. Through 1975 the regional government had contributed about 450 million francs to the new towns, including 365.6
million for highways and 84.5 million to assist with loan repayments.

Despite the presence of national ministries at the local level and the
creation of regional authorities, the 38,000 communes in France have
a strong impact on urban development. By legal theory the localities
have no inherent authority; all power is vested in the national
government, including the right to abolish or modify local governments. Local officials are technically agents of the national government and must report to the minister of interior. The reality is quite
different from the legal abstractions. Over the centuries the government has delegated a good deal of authority to the departments and
communes. Although the government legally could take back those
powers, political support could never be mustered for a major
readjustment. The relatively modest reforms associated with the new
towns program represent the extreme to which change can be pushed
in the French system.

Local authorities, especially communes, thus plan a major role in
the urban development process, as they do in the United States.
Communes have the responsibility for providing schools, roads,
swimming pools, sewage plants, police, and other social services.
However, the most important power held by communes, as well as
departments, is the right to issue building permits for all projects. No
one can build without a permit from the two local governments.

In the communes, the elected mayor is responsible for issuing the
building permits. This right is strongly guarded by the communes.
Without the power to issue building permits they would be over-
whelmed by the national government and private developers. Having
the power, they can successfully oppose new construction through the
refusal to issue the required permit. As a result, large-scale projects
of national interest, including the new towns, can be stopped by
hostile local authorities. The new towns planners could not "steam-
roll" the local authorities as in Britain. Although the government can
strip the communes of the right to issue building permits, political
support for such a move is hopelessly inadequate. The only alternative
is for the planners to work with the communes in the new towns
development process.

The situation is different in the departments, where policy decisions
are made primarily by the missions of civil servants from the various
national ministries, not by elected officials. Whereas at the commune
level the mayor issues the permit, at the department level the
representative of the minister of equipment, the DDE, rather than the

prefect, does it. The rationale for this difference is that the mayor is elected while the prefect of the department is appointed by the minister of interior. As long as the executive function at the departmental level is controlled by appointed officials, questions requiring the technical expertise of urban development officials should be answered by representatives of the ministry of equipment, not the ministry of interior, which appoints the prefect.

The representatives of the DDE are generally closely related to the building industry; they have come from the same educational background as the private developers and are frequently classmates. Many DDE heads have the ambition of escaping from the government with lucrative private sector jobs. This change is called ''getting the slipper'': to secure a successful and financially rewarding position in private industry. The way to achieve the recognition needed to receive such a private sector offer is to help arrange for a successful large-scale project within the territory of concern. Thus, because of their training and financial incentive, the DDE representatives are inclined to promote development for reasons other than national plans.

Many of the DDE's are hostile to the new towns despite the fact that the ministry of equipment has been the main supporter of new towns at the national level. The new towns represent a threat to the DDE's, because the projects preempt the DDE's ability to influence the location of new growth. In effect, one section of the equipment ministry is in conflict with the interests of another. The new towns development process excludes the DDE's from most decisions.

Although local governments have acquired considerable legal responsibility for urban development, they lack the financial means and technical expertise to do very much without national government support. Because of the pattern of financing, it is fair to say that urban growth policy is largely developed at the national level. The government has increasingly sought to establish such a policy through its priorities of investment in new projects.

Despite the financial and technical power wielded by the national government, French local authorities, like their American counterparts, can successfully oppose undesired development simply by refusing to apply for the grants or to give the building permit. A comparable situation exists in the United States, where local authorities must initiate requests for certain federal funds. In France the local authorities will be backed up by the ministry of interior, which resists the attempts by other governmental agencies to ''railroad'' local authorities. The implementation of urban growth policies is thus difficult because both the national and local governments exercise

primarily negative powers. The national government can block a
project by refusing to subsidize it, while the local authorities can
block a project by refusing to apply for funding or to grant a building
permit.

For the French new towns supporters, the development of a
workable administration required securing a balance between two
conflicting claims. The creation of new towns was clearly a national
responsibility. Only the national government has a sufficiently broad
perspective to identify appropriate locations for new towns and
adequate funds. However, given the realities of the French situation,
the cooperation of local authorities was essential to the successful
launching of new towns. The task, therefore, was to establish an
administrative structure in which local authorities had enough voice
in the decision-making process to be satisfied but not enough voice to
sabotage the projects.

The local governments are wary of the new towns policy for a
variety of reasons. First, the construction of new towns, directed by
national planners, represents a threat to their power. For those
authorities located on the site of the new towns, the threat is
understandable. Where new towns are not located, it is less clear.
The new towns policy could infringe on the ability of local authorities
elsewhere to exercise an option concerning the nature and amount of
growth within their own boundaries. The power of each commune to
decide its own growth rate is jealously guarded by communal officials
through issuing building permits. The rapid growth of a new town is
based not only on investments and positive inducements to attract
people and enterprises but also on negative constraints to discourage
construction elsewhere, so that development is concentrated in the
new town. Local authorities where building is to be discouraged
dislike losing their discretionary power over whether development
will take place. It is important to emphasize that local officials are not
unhappy with the prospect of slow growth in their commune, but
rather with the loss of their power to set that rate of growth.
Ironically, although local officials don't want to be forced to maintain
a policy that restricts growth in the commune, that is exactly what the
majority adopt anyway, given the choice.

The majority of the communes discourage large-scale growth
because they lack the financial resources to provide the supporting
services that new residents demand. Government grants and loans
are needed to supplement revenues raised locally. Consequently,
fiscally prudent communes are constrained by the need to repay the
loans. As in America, local authorities welcome new businesses
because they contribute more in taxes than they demand in services,

but the authorities do not want new housing because of the strain on public services caused by new residents. The most notable exception to this pattern is in communist-controlled communes, where local officials support new housing and services as a matter of social policy. These communes would therefore have higher taxes and debts.

Organized cooperation among local authorities in France is more difficult than in the United States. Although communes have agreed in the past jointly to undertake some specific project, such as sewer lines, there is less precedent in France for the cooperation needed to build new towns than in the United States, where there are many special purpose districts encompassing more than one local government. Furthermore, local governments in France exhibit a wider range of political views than those in the United States. It is not uncommon for one commune to have Gaullist officials and an adjacent one to have communists. These officials usually make decisions on narrow ideological grounds. For example, the amount of high-rise apartments as opposed to single-family houses is debated along party lines. The left favors apartment houses because they promote uniformity, equality, and a spirit of collective living. The right supports the aspirations of families to own their own homes and property.

In view of the local government structure in France it is remarkable that a workable administrative structure has been created (table 2–1). To build the new towns, two new organizations have been created at the local level, the Etablissement Public d'Aménagement (development corporation), and the Syndicat Communautaire d'A-ménagement (union of communes for new town development).

Etablissement Public d'Aménagement

Instead of a unitary, all-powerful, British-style development corporation, the French established development corporations with powers limited to certain areas of the development process. One development corporation, called an Etablissement Public d'Aménagement (EPA), is created for each new town. For the nine current new towns, EPA's were established between 1970 and 1973.

The EPA is directed by a board of management, appointed by the minister of equipment. The board includes seven representatives of the communes, departments, and regions, and seven representatives of national ministries, including equipment, interior, finance, and cultural affairs. The president of the board is a local government official. The EPA staff includes engineers, architects, planners, and economists. The technical head of the EPA—the director general—is

Table 2–1. Division of Administrative Responsibilities in the French New Towns

Function	Who Does It?	Who Pays?
planning	at first: MEA Later: EPA	grants from the Ministry of Equipment
land acquisition	EPA, through negotiations or condemnation.	about 50% grants from the Ministry of Equipment and 50% loans from the CDC repaid from sale or leasing of the land
site preparation (utilities, open space, roads, etc.)	EPA	grants from the ministries of Equipment and Interior and loans from the CDC; the exact division depends on the particular project
housing: low income	nonprofit developers (public or private)	1% loans from the CDC
middle income	private developers (limited profits)	a variety of government loans and/or guarantees
upper income	private developers	private sources
employment	private developers: EPA negotiates with potential employers	private sources, although government subsidies or lower taxes are sometimes available
shopping	private developers, after negotiations with EPA	private sources
social services (schools, police, hospitals, recreation, swimming pools, daycare centers, etc.)	SCA	local taxes; loans from the CDC; and grants from the ministries of National Education, Health, Sports, etc.; the exact division depends on the individual project

usually an engineer or economist. Although each EPA is structured somewhat differently, the organization for Saint-Quentin-en-Yvelines (fig. 2–2) is typical. The agency is divided into four units: administration, operations, research and studies, and the town center. As many as one hundred people work for the EPA, some of whom are on loan from regional or national agencies to provide additional technical expertise.

The EPA has two main functions—planning and land development. Planning involves carrying out any needed town planning, development and infrastructure studies; organizing and coordinating land transactions and initial development work; and drawing up cost

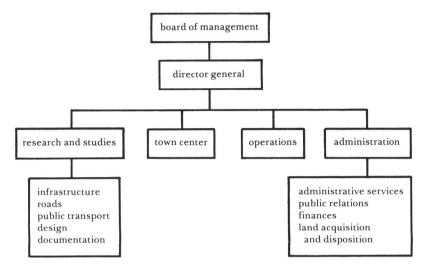

Figure 2-2. Organization of the Etablissement Public d'Aménagement (EPA) at Saint-Quentin-en-Yvelines. Each EPA is organized somewhat differently, but this model is typical. The larger EPA's have over 100 employees.

estimates under the overall program and the timetable for building the new town. Land development concerns include the acquisition of land by power of eminent domain or through negotiations; the development of road, utilities, and other infrastructures; and reselling or leasing land to private or public builders.

Prior to the invention of the EPA concept in 1970, planning in the new towns was undertaken by Missions d'Etudes et d'Aménagement (MEA), planning and research commissions established by the prime minister on April 4, 1966. The MEA's were financed by a special grant in the fifth national plan, which provided thirty million francs per year between 1966 and 1970. The new town master plans were begun and in several cases completed by the MEA staffs.

The MEA's were unable to undertake any development activities in addition to planning. They were legally prevented from buying or selling land. In the Paris region a special agency had been established by the regional government to acquire land, install utilities, and sell it to builders and developers. This agency was the Agence Foncière et Technique de la Région Parisienne (AFTRP). However, reliance on AFTRP was not convenient for the timely development of the new towns. The MEA's were expected to establish the priorities for land acquisition and site preparation while AFTRP actually financed and organized the work. The situation was unsatisfactory, because AFTRP had many other demands placed on it in addition to the new towns.

The EPA took over the MEA staff and functions with additional powers. The EPA's, though, are not all-powerful bodies like the British development corporations. In fact, they are more comparable to the U.S. local urban renewal agencies, which buy and sell land in the cities and negotiate with private developers actually to build structures. Like U.S. urban renewal agencies, the EPA is funded primarily by the national government but is subject to both local and national government control. The EPA's function in the new town development process is that of prime developer. After the plans have been drawn up, it enters the land market. It buys land at a low cost, equips it, and resells it to private developers for construction of houses or commercial buildings. The exception is the land in the town center, which the EPA's generally lease rather than sell.

The EPA divides the new town into smaller districts to be developed by the private sector. These districts are called Zones d'Aménagement Concerté (ZAC), concerted developed zones. The ZAC procedure, created in 1967, is basically a contract between any public authority, such as the EPA, and a private developer concerning the distribution of costs and responsibilities for developing the designated area. The district can be residential or industrial, rehabilitation or new construction. As of 1974, sixty-three residential ZAC's were created in the EPA territory of the five new towns in the Paris region, with an eventual capacity of 161,000 dwellings, according to the contracts between the developers and the EPA's.

Syndicat Communautaire d'Aménagement

If the communal boundaries were large enough to permit the development of a large project within one commune, many of the administrative problems associated with the new towns process could have been avoided. In a couple of cases, such as Créteil and Toulouse-le-Mirail, large-scale projects have been undertaken within the boundaries of only one unusually large commune. Despite the fact that many of the planning goals of these projects coincide with that of the new towns, they are not considered new towns because the national government did not intervene in the development process organized by the local authority. The small number of such communes precludes widespread use of this strategy. The nine designated new towns encompass 114 communes, ranging from four at Berre and Evry to twenty-one for Marne-la-Vallée and twenty-three at L'Isle d'Abeau. American planners can appreciate the problems of coordination when more than one local government is to be included in a project.

This problem was recognized by national planners as far back as the fifth national plan in 1966. The fifth plan states that,

> No coherent development of a [new town] project is possible because of the entanglement of ancient communal limits: the commercial center constructed in A would be supported by people in commune B. In sum, each commune is induced to act according to its own interests, by demanding a commercial center and industrial zone while leaving to its neighbors the costly equipment.

> Most often the opposition [to new towns] becomes irreconcilable: devoid of means, overwhelmed by the size of the problems, afraid of the leap into the unknown that will upset their voters and budget, the communes seem condemned to adopt a negative attitude [toward new towns].[6]

The obvious solution to the local government problem was to combine the small communes into one large local authority for each new town. According to the fifth plan,

> It has appeared for several years now that the only administrative solution is to isolate the relevant zone from the existing communes . . . . The territory necessary for the creation of the "new town" would thus be detached from existing communes in order to be constructed as a new commune. This would be directed by a provisional administration during the first years of construction. Then the new inhabitants would elect a municipal council in the normal manner. This solution is the only one that permits the protection in every possible way of the interests of the existing communes (they would lose a part of their territory but would escape the financial and political consequences arising from the new project); rapid participation by the new inhabitants in directing their own affairs; and especially, the unification of responsibilities, an overall view of the project, and the creation of a clear and coherent financial structure.[7]

However, local authorities and the minister of interior not surprisingly opposed the idea of combining the existing communes into one new one. The elimination of communes would have caused the elimination of some jobs. The problem of achieving a simple administrative reform was summarized by Delouvrier:

> Our communes in France are too small and have more power than the British local authorities. Our new towns in fact are spread over several communes. A new administrative tool was needed to facilitate the creation of the new towns. Although the government of General de Gaulle gave support for such a policy (without which nothing would have been

[6]"Extraits du rapport général de la Commission de l'Equipement Urbain du Vème Plan," mimeographed, my translation, pp. 2–3.

[7]Ibid.

possible), many obstacles were raised, particularly by the minister of interior, who is very traditional and did not want to upset local officials. One solution would have been to force the communes in the new towns to merge into a single new commune. The municipal council could include at first representatives of the existing residents, so that when the new inhabitants arrived they would find a normally operating commune. But that was not possible, because the minister of interior didn't have the courage to say that five or six mayors would be killed off each year. [8]

Instead, the National Assembly in 1970 passed the "Loi Boscher," named after the senator who at the time was also mayor of Evry, which gave local authorities the choice of three procedures — the Ensemble Urbain, the Syndicat Communautaire d'Aménagement, or the Communauté Urbain.

Once the government has designated the zone for the new town development, the communes within it have four months to choose one of the three alternatives. If after four months the communes can't reach an agreement among themselves or if after another four months the communes still can't reach an agreement with the EPA concerning the precise distribution of responsibilities for developing the new town, then the national government can impose its choice.

The Ensemble Urbain is the simplest method of local government reform. All of the communes in the new town are simply combined into one new commune, as advocated by Delouvrier. The old communes cease to exist, with residents voting for representatives of the large new commune. The only exception is that for the first few years of development a nine-person municipal council is appointed by the government. The residents vote for three councillors after 2,000 dwellings are occupied and three each two and four years after the first three. At this point the council would have eighteen members, one-half elected and one-half appointed. Within three years of this point the entire eighteen-member council must be elected in the normal way by the citizens. Only one new town, Le Vaudreuil, has selected this method of local government reform.

In response to local government opposition, the Loi Boscher provided two other choices, each of which preserves the existing local authorities. In 1968, the Association of French Mayors, representing the communes' views, proposed the Syndicat Communautaire d'A-ménagement (SCA), the community syndicate for development. The territory to be developed for the new town is detached from the existing communes and combined into a new area, called the Zone d'Agglomération Nouvelle (ZAN). Usually one part of a commune is inside the ZAN and another part is outside. For example, an existing small town could be excluded from the ZAN. Some communes have

[8] Interview with Paul Delouvrier, July 1974, my translation.

chosen to place their entire territory inside the ZAN rather than just the part to be developed.

The old communes do not disappear with the creation of the SCA. The ZAN is like a commune only from a budget and tax standpoint. Voters still elect councillors according to the old communal boundaries. The SCA, composed of representatives from the municipal council of each of the participating communes, manages the tax system and budget of the new town territory. This is like administering a joint estate consisting only of property acquired after marriage. Construction of the new town is taken over jointly by all communes through the SCA, with all relevant income and expenditures equally apportioned.

The SCA has no powers outside the area of concern unless a particular commune prefers otherwise. Inside the ZAN the old communes continue to perform routine functions (police, vital statistics, etc.). For tax purposes the ZAN is regarded as an additional commune. Local taxes are uniform inside the ZAN, with the rates established by the SCA, not the individual communes. The communal facilities needed for the new towns are based on a single budget voted by the SCA and financed by uniform tax rates and loans from the national government. Outside the ZAN each commune sets its own rate. Local taxes collected outside the ZAN are not used to pay for the new town. In this way, existing residents do not pay higher taxes to support the new town. The SCA has a small technical staff to review the EPA work. However, the SCA lacks sufficient resources to hire adequate experts. It therefore relies on the local representatives of the ministries and the EPA for technical work.

The SCA is like a miniparliament. It usually comprises two members from each participating commune, unless one commune has a significantly larger population at the time of designation. SCA representatives are selected by the various communal councils rather than by direct election. The SCA members are invariably also on the communal councils.

For all the administrative complexity, the long-term effect of the SCA system is merely to postpone the inevitable. According to the 1970 law, after twenty-five years (during the 1990s), the ZAN will be converted to a normal commune. The SCA system, therefore, delays the total liquidation of existing communes well beyond the likely terms of office of current politicians. For the moment, the reforms have been aimed at the top priority—the creation of a workable financial structure consistent with French local government tradition. The role of local officials has not been reduced, only channeled into the SCA forum, where power is shared with other officials from other communes.

Seven of the nine new towns have chosen the SCA. Cergy-Pontoise, Evry, Saint-Quentin-en-Yvelines, and L'Isle d'Abeau have one SCA each. Melun-Sénart has three SCA's, because development is taking place in three discontinuous sectors. The EPA has written three master plans, each approved by the SCA concerned. Marne-la-Vallée has also been subdivided into three sectors, corresponding to three points of development. However, only one of these has an SCA, because the government has not yet officially declared the other two sectors to be part of the new town. At Berre, development is also planned for three isolated spots — northwest, southwest, and east of the Bay of Berre. The northwest sector has an SCA; the eastern part contains only one commune and therefore doesn't need an SCA. The southwest part of the new town is not being developed by the EPA or SCA. Instead, the three communes concerned have been permitted to manage development through an intercommunal agreement, called a Syndicat Intercommunal à Vocations Multiples (SIVOM).

The third alternative is the Communauté Urbain. This is a limited form of regional government, extending over a wider territory than just a new town. The communes in an urban area can agree among themselves to cooperate in the provision of needed services and facilities. A regional assembly is then elected by the participating communes to decide on priorities and uniform financing for the area. The communes within a new town could choose to place responsibility for the development of the new town in the hands of the Communauté Urbain if such an organization exists in the region. This arrangement eliminates the requirement for the communes within the new town to form an SCA but places the risks and responsibilities for the development of the new town on all the communes of the region, not just those within the new town borders.

One of the nine new towns, Lille-Est, is directed by a Communauté Urbain. In addition, the three communes where most new construction will occur agreed among themselves to combine into one new commune, called Ascq. This system has proved a mixed blessing. On the one hand, the Communauté Urbain method provides the new town with a larger base from which to draw the required local share of development costs. On the other hand, the Communauté Urbain considers the new town to be primarily a regional not a national concern. Because the new town was initiated by the choice of an existing local authority and not imposed on reluctant local authorities as in other new towns, the Communauté Urbain tends to feel less need to conform to the uniform standards and policies established by the national government. One trivial yet highly symbolic manifestation of the relative independence of the new town in the Lille area is a long-running dispute over the name. The national government designated the new town "la Ville Nouvelle de Lille-Est," with the Etablissement Public known as EPALE (Etablissement Public d'Aménagement de Lille-Est). However, the Communauté Urbain calls it "Villeneuve d'Ascq." Although "Ville Nouvelle" and Villeneuve" both translate as "new town," the different terms are significant in French. "Ville Nouvelle" is the name selected by the national government to emphasize the uniqueness of the nine projects in terms of government support, as compared to other new urban development projects. "Villeneuve" is a less lofty description, one that has been selected through the centuries by communes that elsewhere in France have joined together of their own volition into a new commune.

Relations between the EPA and SCA are not ideal. Local officials naturally harbor a good deal of mistrust about the outside planners coming in. On the other hand, planners tend to be impatient with the local authorities, who do not have the technical expertise to manage properly the complexities of a large-scale rapid development process. According to Boscher, who observed both sides of the relationship as the first president of the SCA and EPA for Evry, some of the technical planners are "apt to consider themselves as if they were in the wild jungles of Africa and have nothing else in front of them but a few savage people." The planners suffer from the occupational hazard of imposing technical solutions without always understanding the specific actors involved. The new towns in particular offer a golden opportunity for planners to put forth projects that would be rejected in a built-up town.

Local officials frequently delay EPA projects by insisting on lengthy hearings. The issues that interest them are usually matters such as which developer will be awarded a particular contract. Local officials who are close to a particular developer may question the choice made by the EPA and try to secure a change to a more "sympathetic" developer who has had dealings with them in the past. Other local officials may try to stop projects because they are not seen to be in the best interest of the existing residents. An example of this would be the insertion of single-family houses in a working class commune. The job of smoothing the relations between the local officials and planners frequently must be done at the top, among the technical head of the EPA, the political head of the EPA, and the head of the SCA. The last two jobs are sometimes held by one individual to simplify the process.

Many local officials are hopelessly over their heads. Whenever a district of several hundred is suddenly flooded with tens of thousands of new residents the officials selected by the old residents are unlikely to reflect accurately the needs and interests of the new ones. One example was cited by Boscher in Evry:

> The neighboring village of Courcouronnes, which is now three or four thousand strong, was a village of exactly 152 inhabitants [in 1971]. That the new town council, which was elected in 1971 by the eighty-two adult inhabitants of that day, theoretically represents the 3,500 of today is of course a complete fallacy. It is also quite obvious that the poor devils, who are intellectually under the average, will be chucked out in 1977 when the next general municipal council election comes up.[9]

In fact, the local government elections of 1977 changed many of the new town communes. As in the rest of France, the new towns voters elected leftist local officials. The pace of development of new towns was slowed for a while as the new officials reevaluated projects and priorities proposed by the EPA.

Despite the intensely political nature of local government officials, the new towns have not been opposed by either the left or the right. The left, while wary of a policy initiated by a right-wing national government, has not criticized the new towns because they see the program as beneficial to their constituents. The right, though uneasy with the concentration of left-wing voters in new towns, has not opposed the projects because they were proposed by their national government.

A few of the new towns were located in areas where communes with left- and right-wing sympathies existed side by side. The problem of combining communist and Gaullist politicians has been acute. One response has been the exclusion of the communes with left-wing views from the area of active new town construction efforts and from the SCA. This strategy was used at Evry and to a lesser extent at Saint-Quentin-en-Yvelines. At Evry the new town zones for the EPA and SCA were considerably reduced from the original study area. The reason was that the most ardent local advocate of the new town was the mayor of Evry and deputy for the district, Michel Boscher. The original fourteen communes of the study area were reduced to four, all of which were controlled at the time by Gaullist supporters, and the communist communes were eliminated by the government from the EPA and SCA zone. As long as the government had the choice of which communes to invite or compel to join the

[9]Interview with Michel Boscher, June 1974.

SCA, the practical course of action was to remove the irreconcilably hostile communes rather than to force them into unions that the opponents would try hard to sabotage. At Saint-Quentin-en-Yvelines the largest commune, Trappes, for which the town was originally to be named, voted to stay out of the SCA, although its communist mayor, Hugo, participates in the SCA.

The other alternative is to create more than one SCA. At Berre in particular the project is divided into two SCA's, one comprising left-wing communes and the other right-wing. This strategy can be justified on physical grounds because the areas to be urbanized at Berre, as well as the other two new towns with more than one SCA—Marne-la-Vallée and Melun-Sénart—are discontinuous. One SCA covers each area of development. Because of these politically motivated adjustments the boundaries of the various agencies concerned with the new towns frequently do not coincide. There are three basic territorial definitions of the new towns. The first is .the original study area for the EPA, or its predecessor, the MEA. This was the area within which planning studies were conducted. Most of the material generated in the 1960s used these boundaries. The study areas of the Paris new towns ranged in size from 50,000 at Cergy-Pontoise to 200,000 at Evry. The provincial new town sites contained fewer residents. The second definition is the zone of operations for the EPA, the area in which it acquires and improves land. This area is considerably smaller than the original study area in Evry and Saint-Quentin-en-Yvelines. At Evry the original studies were conducted in a fourteen-commune area containing 200,000 people, while actual development work has been limited to a five-commune area containing 33,000 people. The area of concern at Saint-Quentin-en-Yvelines was reduced from twenty-five communes with 119,000 people to eleven communes with 41,000 inhabitants. The EPA areas for the nine new towns were fixed between 1969–73 (see table 2–2). The third definition of the new town boundaries is the ZAN area, fixed when the SCA or Ensemble Urbain was created. The population in the ZAN is small, because the ZAN normally contains the undeveloped part of the communes (see table 2–3). At the time of designation the Paris new town ZAN's ranged in size from 368 in the SCA for Marne-la-Vallée sector 2 to 23,863 in Saint-Quentin-en-Yvelines. (See fig. 2–3.)

The complex administrative structure has contributed to the construction delays experienced by the French new towns. The French planners would have preferred the British method of creating a development corporation to oversee virtually all aspects of new town

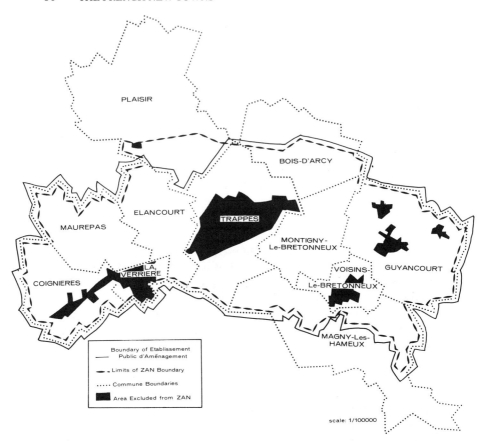

Figure 2–3. Administrative boundaries of Saint-Quentin-en-Yvelines. The map indicates the diversity in definitions of the new town boundaries. The new towns are not located in isolated areas surrounded by green belts. The ZAN, where development is concentrated, generally does not have a large existing population, although a commune has the choice of joining the ZAN in its entirety rather than detaching only its undeveloped portion for the ZAN. In Saint-Quentin-en-Yvelines, as the map indicates, some communes joined the new town completely and others only partially.

construction. However, France like the United States, requires that local governments be included in the development process. American planners have concluded that a national new towns policy is impossible with strong local governments. Such critics should consider the following points: (*a*) France has far more local authorities per capita

Table 2–2. Population in the New Town Study and Development Areas

Town	Original Study Area		EPA Area		
	Number of Communes	Population in 1968	Number of Communes	Population in 1968	Population in 1975
Paris region					
Cergy-Pontoise	16	60,000	16	53,445	84,487
Evry	14	200,000	4	33,180	53,673
Marne-la-Vallée	25	100,000	21	69,878	81,624
Melun-Sénart	18	80,000	18	65,709	94,548
Saint-Quentin-en-Yvelines	25	85,000	11	41,415	103,655
Total Paris region	*98*	*525,000*	*70*	*263,627*	*417,987*
Provinces					
Etang-de-Berre	7	100,000	4	76,766	120,602
L'Isle d'Abeau	24	40,000	23	38,213	47,573
Lille-Est	9	30,000	9	26,288	38,600
Le Vaudreuil	8	15,000	8	6,320	7,162
Total provinces	*48*	*185,000*	*44*	*147,587*	*213,937*

or per square mile than the United States; (*b*) the French new towns contain both right-wing and communist-governed communes; and (*c*) France has a much weaker tradition of cooperation among local authorities than the United States, where special purpose districts are common. Similarly, American local authorities have historically been able to expand their boundaries through annexation far more easily than French communes.

The existence of new towns today in France is a testimony to the triumph of determined national policy over major administrative obstacles. Faced with the need to provide a significant role for the local authorities in the new towns development process, the French have created a complex administrative structure that ''saves face'' for existing local officials while providing adequate, if not inspiring, local authority support for the new towns development process. Local officials have secured their most important objectives: they have not been removed from office and they have retained their major power, the right to issue construction permits. The new towns planners have secured their most important objective: the creation of a uniform tax base so that the new town can be planned as a single entity rather than as a collection of competing communes.

Table 2-3. Local Governments in the New Towns

Town	Type of Government	Date Created	Number of Communes	Population at Designation
Paris region				
Cergy-Pontoise	SCA	12/18/72	15	5,231
Evry	SCA	11/29/73	5	2,413
Marne-la-Vallée				
sector 1	none created		3[a]	
sector 2	SCA	12/14/72	6	368
sector 3	none created		12[a]	
Melun-Sénart				
Sénart-Villeneuve	SCA	8/9/73	4	12,406
Rogeau-Sénart	SCA	10/9/74	7	2,081
Grand-Melun	SCA	1/24/74	7	242
Saint-Quentin-en-Yvelines	SCA	12/21/72	11	23,863
Total Paris region			70	45,686
Provinces				
Etang-de-Berre				
Northwest	SCA	12/18/72	3	31,160
Southwest	none created		3[a]	
Vitrolles	none needed[b]		1	5,058
L'Isle d'Abeau	SCA	12/26/72	21	12,575
Lille-Est	1 new commune + Communauté Urbain	2/25/70	1[a]	26,288
Le Vaudreuil	Ensemble Urbain	12/11/72	8	438
Total provinces			37	75,519
Total new towns			107	121,205

[a]Number of communes likely to be included in a ZAN in the future
[b]Only one commune is found in the sector

3
ECONOMICS OF
THE FRENCH NEW TOWNS

New towns are extremely complex economic structures. Many aspects have been explored, but no study has yet provided a comprehensive picture. There are two major economic issues, especially for American observers. First, are new towns cheaper or more expensive than other forms of urban development? Second, how can new towns be financed successfully in a free-market economy? It is remarkable that in the voluminous literature on new towns neither question has been answered; the first issue in particular has been neglected. Several studies have attempted to compare the costs of various projects or of one function in a variety of settings, but no one has put together a definitive answer. Models are not available to help analyze data. No definitive answer to the question can be given here either, but some preliminary and tentative conclusions can be drawn concerning the economic competitiveness of the French new towns.

The second issue has also been left unanswered. To American supporters and critics alike, the financial obstacles are the most serious problems facing the new towns. For the critics, the financial difficulties experienced by publicly and privately sponsored new towns demonstrate the weakness of the technique. American supporters dispair at their inability to launch a financially strong new town. During the 1960s they could point to Columbia, Maryland, as a financially successful new town, but even that project has suffered in recent years.

All new projects require ''up-front'' costs to be paid in advance of receiving revenue. Money is needed for the acquisition of land, the installation of infrastructure, and the construction of buildings. When these buildings are finished they are sold or rented at a price that enables the developer to cover the costs incurred at the beginning. Because new towns are very large-scale projects, more up-front expenses are incurred. Apparently, only the national government has the financial resources to guide large projects such as new towns through the early stages.

The British instituted a simple financing system. The development corporation, which is responsible for virtually all aspects of the development process, borrows money from the National Treasury. These fifty-year loans are repaid with the assets received from land sales or rents. The American new town program has relied on private financial initiatives. HUD has provided loan guarantees to private developers so that they could secure loans in the private market at lower interest rates. The additional cost from delays and administration incurred by private developers, however, almost completely negated the benefits from lower cost loans. Uncertainties as to the total amount of up-front costs required and the time period for repayment have rendered the American system unworkable. The French system of financing is as complex as the administrative structure discussed in the previous chapter. It deserves the attention of American new towns planners because it has achieved the objective that has so far eluded the Americans: a rational distribution of the financial burden among the national government, the local authorities, and the private sector.

Before considering the more theoretical question of comparative costs of urban development between new towns and other alternatives, this chapter will explain the procedures for public financial support of the new towns in France. The next chapter will examine the role of private enterprise in the French new towns development process.

FINANCING THE FRENCH NEW TOWNS

The previous chapter demonstrated that the French have installed a complex administrative structure because local governments have the legal authority but not the financial capacity to build new towns. Administrative responsibilities were divided among the local authorities, national ministries, private developers, and development corporations (EPA).

Each member of the development team is expected to make a financial contribution to the new town. The local authority builds public facilities, such as schools and daycare centers, and provides public services, such as police and welfare. These functions are paid for by local taxes, national grants, and loans from the CDC. The EPA conducts studies, buys the land, installs infrastructure and secures developers. These activities are financed by grants and loans from the government and by receipts from land sales. I shall examine in more detail the financial operations of these actors.

Syndicat Communautaire d'Aménagement

The SCA has the same taxing powers as any other commune in France. Local authorities must receive money for two basic purposes. First, funds are needed for overhead expenses arising from day-to-day functioning (salaries for public employees, maintenance of public buildings, etc.). The second category is the money needed for investment in the new facilities for a rapidly growing community, such as schools, day care centers, and sports facilities.

Overhead expenses are financed by locally produced revenues. The SCA, like other communes in France, has two basic types of local taxes, one levied directly by the local authorities and the other returned by the national or regional government.

Direct local taxes — The SCA's, like other communes, collect taxes from four different sources: (1) a tax on improved property (*taxe fonciere des propriétés bâties*); (2) a property tax on unimproved land (*taxe foncière des propriétées nonbâties*); (3) a tax paid by the occupant, based on the number of rooms in his house or apartment (for example, 400 francs for two rooms, 1000 francs for five rooms) (*taxe d'habitation*); and (4) a tax paid by the employer, based on the value of his factory or enterprise (*taxe professionelle*).[1] The tax rate is established annually by the SCA for each of the four types. By far the biggest generator of local income is the tax on employers, which accounts for over half of the total raised locally. The housing tax raises about one-fourth, the tax on improved land one-fifth, and the tax on unimproved land 1 percent.[2]

The property tax is frequently waived under the new ZAC method of development. As part of the agreement between the local authority and the private developer, the tax is not paid for several years in exchange for a financial contribution at the time of development to help meet the cost of building new public services. To make up for some of the lost revenues, the national government makes a contribution to the commune. This rebate is called the *subvention fiscale*

---

[1] In 1974 the system was changed slightly. The *taxe foncière des propriétés bâties* and *nonbâties* were previously known as the *contribution foncière des propriétés bâties* and *nonbâties*. The *taxe d'habitation* was previously the *contribution mobilière*, while the *taxe professionelle* was previously the *patente*.

[2] Although the local authorities set their own tax rates, they do not actually collect taxes themselves. The national government collects both the national and local taxes and returns the local portion back to the communes.

automatisué (SFA), or *recettes à attendre de la subvention compensa- tice pour l'exonération du foncier bâti.*

Revenue sharing—The *versement représentatif de la taxe sur la salaire* (VRTS) is a payroll tax paid by employers and collected throughout France by the national government. The state then allocates the money to localities according to the two criteria of population and local tax effort. The larger the population and the more the commune collects in taxes, the more it receives in VRTS. In the Paris region a special redistribution called the *fond d'égalisation des charges* (FEC) is used. This system removes one-third of the VRTS and redistributes it to the communes by a three-factor method that includes the first two factors plus local income. The poorer suburban jurisdictions in the Paris region thus benefit from the reallocation, while central Paris contributes more than it receives. About sixteen billion francs is collected in France each year under VRTS, of which six hundred million goes to the Paris region.

As rapidly growing areas, new towns require more than their "fair share" of revenue. If the VRTS were computed strictly on the basis of current population, the new towns would suffer because the existing population inside the SCA area is small. The population used to calculate the percentage of revenue returned to the new towns is an artificial one (*population fictive*). It is derived by multiplying the number of houses under construction by six and adding that figure to the real population.[3]

The SCA's have not had any major problems in meeting overhead expenses with locally generated taxes. Although expenses have increased each year growth in population and nonresidential activities has permitted the SCA's to generate additional income. The tax rates have therefore not increased. For example, the average local taxes paid by residents of the five Paris new towns was 281 francs per person in 1974 and 272 francs in 1975. In comparison, the average tax per person in all suburban communes of the Paris region with more than 10,000 residents was 290 francs in 1975. These figures encompass the household tax (*taxe d'habitation*), the residential portion of the property tax, and the percentage of the national grants in lieu of local taxes attributable to residential property. While the SCA's have been able to meet day-to-day overhead costs with local revenues, resources are woefully inadequate to finance the construction of needed new public facilities. The SCA must therefore turn to outside sources of funding to pay for new construction.

[3] For the purpose of computing the *population fictive* it is assumed that there are six persons per household in the new towns. That figure was not chosen to reflect sociological realities but to give the new towns an additional benefit in computing the rebate. This is another example of how the French system provides for a high degree of

The problem facing the SCA is a typical one for local authorities in France. The government and local authorities together perpetuate the myth that the communes are financially self-sufficient. This belief permits the communes to maintain a stance of independence from national control and permits the national government to minimize direct financial contribution to the localities. In reality, the amount of revenue produced by local taxes can't pay for new projects. A commune that is not growing can meet its expenses, mainly maintenance and salaries. Jurisdictions where new services and facilities are required to meet the needs of an expanding population, such as new town, cannot afford them.

Historically, local authorities financed new investments by securing loans, principally from the Caisse des Dépôts et Consignations (CDC). The relationship between the CDC and local authorities is not like the typical lender and borrower; there has traditionally been no limit to the supply, for the CDC always had more than enough funds to lend money to any local authority. Long-term loans were made to the local authorities at negligible interest rates. In view of the demographic and economic stagnation in France until recent years the system never failed. Communes made few demands on the CDC, but when they did the money was always available.

In recent years, the communes have not been able to borrow enough funds to pay for all of the new construction required to accommodate the fast-growing and urbanizing population. The CDC has started to charge interest, although still below market rates. The government has increasingly been forced to finance large public works through grants to the localities. These grants are frequently forthcoming only after the commune has borrowed as much as possible. They are either used directly for construction or to pay off debts incurred by the local authority. In an era of rapid growth, local authorities are in a state of perpetual financial chaos.

Through 1975 national grants to the SCA's for the construction of new social facilities totaled around 733.2 million francs. By far the largest share of the money came from the ministry of national education, which has invested around 207.5 million francs for primary schools and 318.1 million for secondary schools. The ministry of sports has contributed 106.4 million francs, with the ministry of health adding 85.7 million for various health and social service facilities. Around 15.5 million francs have been given for cultural and administrative facilities. Around 392 million francs have been spent in the Paris new towns and 341 million in the provincial ones.[4]

---

ad hoc and individual relationships among national and local authorities.

[4]Groupe Central des Villes Nouvelles, *Bilan des villes nouvelles au 31 Décembre 1975* (Paris: Groupe Central des Villes Nouvelles, 1976).

No generalization can be made concerning the percentages of national financial contributions to particular projects. On the average, the national government contributes about one-half of the costs for schools and other cultural and social service facilities, with the other half raised by loans. However, the national ministries have discretion in this matter. The exact split between national and local contributions is flexible and subject to negotiations. For example, official guidelines may indicate that the national government is expected to pay one-half the cost of a new school, but in reality the ministry of national education may provide 70 percent. The distribution of cost between the national government and the local authority will be determined by "unique" circumstances, such as the relative financial strength of the commune, the availability of CDC loans, the strength of national commitment to the particular project, and the interpersonal relations between the representatives of the ministry and the commune.

Repaying loans is the most serious problem facing the SCA's. It means the difference between financial security and chaos. Most loans to the SCA's are for thirty years at 8 percent interest, although some carry lower charges. The SCA's are expected to repay the principal and interest from local taxes. This implies that the increase in locally generated revenues from the expansion of the tax base will be sufficiently large to cover both overhead expenses and loan repayment. In reality, no SCA has reached this position. French planners have therefore been forced to create a complex system that takes care of both the immediate financial problems of the SCA's and the long-term policy of committing the SCA's to repay their loans.

The SCA's have been permitted to defer repayment of the principal or interest on most loans for four years. The first four annuities on the loans are paid instead by the national government, which has contributed 216.8 million francs on behalf of the nine new towns through 1975, and the Paris district, which contributed 84.5 million francs for the five new towns of the Paris region. In 1977, another crisis arose at the end of the four-year period for many of the loans. The SCA's still could not generate enough money from local taxes to start repaying the loans themselves. As a result it became increasingly difficult to borrow money for further projects in the new towns. The CDC was reluctant to lend more money to the new towns in view of their inability to repay the existing loans. The new towns therefore sought financing from other banks. No long-term solution has been found for the problem of paying the local share of new investments. Deferments are continuing on loans already secured, with the national government and the Paris district picking up the tab.

For American new towns the cost of borrowing money is critical. In a free market if someone is able to borrow money at below market rates a subsidy is being made, because that money could have been loaned to someone else at a higher rate. There is, in other words, an opportunity cost associated with lending money at low interest rates. Although the French local authorities are receiving loans at the rather high 8 percent interest rate, the situation is complicated by the system of deferred repayment of loans. Because of the deferments it will be a number of years before a true rate of interest can be computed for the French loans.

Some detailed studies of the financial situation have been made at Cergy-Pontoise, the oldest new town.[5] In 1973, the SCA spent around 4.6 million francs on overhead, including 183,000 francs for debt repayment. Receipts totaled 4.5 million francs, including 2.3 million francs from the VRTS and 1.5 million from direct local taxes. The remaining 700,000 francs were generated by various charges for the use of public facilities and by other miscellaneous methods.

Predictions have been made concerning the financial situation of the Cergy-Pontoise SCA in 1980. There are three sources of uncertainty in such predictions: the pace of construction, the level of inflation, and the arrangements for repaying the debt. The pace of construction affects both the amount of expenditure and the amount of taxes that can be generated. If construction of new public facilities is delayed then the SCA would have to borrow money and therefore make lower repayments. On the other hand, delays in construction mean that there are fewer business and residents to tax and the aggregate property values will be lower. Forecasts were therefore required for the number of new jobs and residents likely to be attracted between 1974 and 1980. Second, the forecasts had to be adjusted for different levels of inflation. The planners used three levels, representing minimal, moderate, and high inflation. The predicted surplus or deficit for 1980 will be accentuated by high inflation. The third factor is the most critical one for the future financial strength of the SCA. Under the sixth plan, repayment of most loans taken out by the SCA does not begin until four years later.

In 1973, for example, the SCA was supposed to pay about 2 million francs in annuities on loans. It actually paid only 183,000 francs, with the rest paid by the region or state. Beginning in 1977 the SCA would be obligated to make the entire 2-million-franc payment itself. Meanwhile, it was uncertain whether loans taken out after 1975 would have the same four-year grace period before the SCA started

[5]Etablissement Public d'Aménagement de la Ville Nouvelle de Cergy-Pontoise, *Etude Du Développement et des perspectives financières du Syndicat Communautaire d'Aménagement de la ville nouvelle de Cergy-Pontoise, 1973–1980* (Cergy-Pontoise: Etablissement Public d'Aménagement de la Ville Nouvelle de Cergy-Pontoise, 1974).

making the annual repayments. If the deferment system continues until 1980 the SCA is not in a bad financial condition. If the deferment stopped, the SCA's finances would be in chaos (see table 3–1). With the deferments, the SCA would show a cumulative profit of around 1.4 million francs in 1980, as a result of building up a surplus of revenues in the late 1970s, to be offset by an increase in expenses in 1980 as the second wave of deferments ends. Without deferments, the SCA is predicted to have a cumulative deficit of 31.6 million by 1980. The long-term financial stability of the SCA's is thus clearly dependent on the degree to which the government permits them to delay repaying the loans they have taken out for the development of public facilities.

Etablissement Public d'Aménagement

Like the SCA, the EPA also has two types of expenses. Both have expenses for overhead, which include personnel, office furniture, and conducting studies and writing plans. But whereas the SCA is responsible for the construction of superstructures, the EPA manages the development of roads, sewers, and other needed infrastructure.

The EPA's budget differs from the SCA's in several respects. The SCA is a local authority that can raise tax revenue and that must

Table 3–1. Annual Budget of Cergy-Pontoise Syndicat Communautaire d'Aménagement (in millions of francs)

Item	1973	1974	1975	1976	1977	1978	1979	1980
Receipts	4.5	8.7	13.1	19.1	24.8	31.2	35.9	42.1
With deferment								
Expenses	4.4	8.7	11.5	13.8	20.1	28.3	37.4	52.8
Loan* repayment	0.2	0.2	0.2	0.4	2.2	3.0	5.3	9.3
Annual balance	0.1	0.0	1.6	5.3	4.7	2.9	-1.5	-10.7
Cumulative balance	0.1	0.1	0.7	6.0	10.7	13.6	12.1	1.4
Without deferment								
Expenses					24.4	35.0	46.5	65.7
Loan* repayment					6.4	9.7	14.4	22.1
Annual balance					0.4	-3.8	-10.6	-23.6
Cumulative balance	0.1	0.1	0.7	6.0	6.4	2.6	-8.0	-31.6

NOTE: Figures beyond 1976 are estimates, based on assumptions concerning the rate of inflation and pace of development. The table shows that if the deferment system continues for the period of the seventh national plan (1976–80) the SCA's cumulative surplus would be 1.4 million francs in 1980. However, if the deferment system is not continued, the SCA would have a debt of 31.6 million francs.

* included in Expenses

answer to an electorate. Budgets are created each year to encompass all project expenditures and receipts for the one-year period. The EPA, as a developer, has no taxing ability. It is concerned with the long term and does not generate a meaningful overall budget for annual income and expenditures. The new town is divided by the EPA into a series of districts called ZAC's, within which virtually all development activities are concentrated. At the time each ZAC is created, a *bilan* (balance sheet) is prepared, showing the amount of investment required and the revenues likely to be generated. Using the ZAC method, EPA finances are global in time but limited in space to one district of the new town; the SCA budget is global in space but limited in time to one year. A meaningful EPA budget therefore must combine individual budgets for the various ZAC's into an annual framework. In addition, the EPA incurs certain expenses that cannot be attributed to a particular ZAC. These must be added to the collection of individual ZAC budgets.

To get through the early years, when expenses are the highest and income lowest, the EPA must rely on outside financing. Funds are provided by two principal sources: grants from the national government and loans from the CDC. Government grants for infrastructure are issued by the ministries of equipment and interior consistent with the goals established in the five-year national plans. The ministry of equipment provides funds for the acquisition of land, the construction of a primary road network, and the development of open space. The ministry of interior supports the installation of primary water and sewer services and, for the provincial new towns, secondary road construction. Basically, the government grants are designed to cover the primary infrastructure development required to connect the ZAC's with each other and the outside world.

Through 1975, the nine new towns have received around 1.6 billion francs for infrastructure in grants from the government, including around 570 million for the provincial new towns and 1.05 billion for the Paris new towns. The two largest grants were from the ministry of equipment for land acquisition and primary roads. The government has provided about 767.2 million francs to buy land (approximately 45 percent of the total acquisition expenses incurred), about 330 million francs of which went to the provincial new towns. The new towns have received about 534.8 million francs for the construction of primary roads (approximately 55 percent of the total cost), with about 125 million going to the provinces and 410 million to the Paris new towns. (The Paris regional government provides the remaining 45 percent, around 365 million francs, to the five new towns in its region.) The third largest category of grants came from the ministry of interior for construction of primary water and sewer services —

about 274.5 million francs, 30 percent to the provincial new towns and 70 percent to the Paris region. Smaller grants have been made to all nine new towns for open space development (21.5 million francs) and to the four provincial new towns for secondary water and sewer services and roads (31.4 million).[6]

In general, the government provides grants for the construction of primary infrastructure, which connects the project area to the outside world. Tertiary infrastructure connects the individual building to the water, sewer, and road systems. These services are normally provided by private builders, who recoup the cost through a surcharge to the buyer, called the *charge foncière*. The secondary infrastructure, which connects the other two, is provided through a contractual arrangement between the EPA and the private builders. The exact division of the cost of secondary infrastructure between the EPA and private builders is subject to negotiations for each project area.

Because the EPA's generally do not receive government grants for the installation of secondary infrastructure, they must generate the rest of the funds required for land development themselves. In the long term, the sale of prepared land to private builders is supposed to cover the cost of secondary infrastructure. Through 1975, land sales had generated 857 million francs, including 735 million in the Paris new towns and 122 million in the provincial ones. Around half of the sales have been to home builders, about 10 percent each for construction of commercial facilities or offices, and the remainder for industry.

To date, expenses have exceeded the receipts generated from land sales. The nine EPA's spent just over two billion francs through 1975, of which 347 million is attributable to the four provincial new towns. The two largest items of expense are land acquisition and the installation of secondary utilities. The nine new towns have been forced to raise 580 million francs for land acquisition in addition to the 767 million francs received in national grants. The secondary infrastructure expenses borne by the EPA's amounted to 701 million francs through 1975. The Paris new towns account for nearly 90 percent of the expenses. Studies, publicity, and personnel salaries cost around 265 million francs. Approximately 71 million francs has been paid for interest on the loans taken out by the EPA's. The remaining expenses were for a variety of specific efforts, such as the provision of temporary housing for construction workers and the construction and management of parking lots. Some of the new towns

[6] Groupe Central des Villes Nouvelles, *Bilan*.

have to pay taxes on part of their revenues, such as the parking lot charges.

The difference between the EPA's expenses and the receipts generated from land sales must be made up primarily through loans. Most loans are secured from the CDC for six years, although a few have been for twenty years. The majority are guaranteed by the Fonds National d'Aménagement Foncier et de l'Urbanisme (FNAFU), the national fund for land development and planning. The FNAFU is an interministerial committee headed by a representative of a division within the ministry of equipment called Direction de l'Aménagement Foncier et de l'Urbanisme (DAFU), the land development and planning administration. The rate at which the CDC usually lends money is 6.75 percent (comparable to a prime interest rate); with FNAFU guarantees, the EPA secures the loans at 3 percent. The EPA also receives financial support from a variety of other sources, including special grants from the ministry of equipment to cover some of the cost of the administration and construction of facilities (such as the parking lots), fees for providing services to other agencies (such as technical planning or architectural expertise), and receipts from operating the parking lots.

If all expenses are totaled, the nine EPA's have spent approximately 4.3 billion francs through 1975 (see table 3–2). This figure, however,

Table 3–2. Financial Statement for the Nine EPA's through 1975 (in millions of francs)

Expenses		Receipts	
Land acquisition	1,347	Land Sales	
		Commercial	94
Primary roads	900	Housing	412
		Industry	259
Primary water and sewer	275	Offices	92
		Grants	
Open space	22	Ministry of Equipment	
Secondary infrastructure	732	Land acquisition	767
		Primary roads	535
Personnel	196	Open space	22
		Ministry of Interior	
Studies	69	Water and sewer	275
		Secondary infrastructure	31
Interest	69	Paris district (for	
		primary roads)	365
Other	404	Other	404
Subtotal	4,014	Subtotal	3,256
Loan repayment	159	Loans	917
Total expenses	4,173	Total receipts	4,173

excludes expenditures for planning, land acquisition, and infrastructure development prior to the creation of the EPA's between 1969 and 1973. The first planning efforts for the new towns were undertaken by regional agencies. In the Paris region, the IAURP was responsible for planning before the MEA's were organized. Land acquisition and site preparation were begun prior to the creation of the EPA's in several new towns, particularly Melun-Sénart. An agency of the regional government, the Agence Foncière et Technique de la Région Parisienne (AFTRP), the Paris region land development agency, carried out the activities because the MEA's were prohibited from doing these things. AFTRP, like the EPA, is a development authority that buys and improves land if the ultimate use of the land is for a public project in the Paris region. Although it could do the same sort of things as the EPA, it was considered unsuitable as the new town developer because there are many other demands on its time and resources.

Some detailed forecasts were made in 1974 of the likely financial statement of the Saint-Quentin-en-Yvelines EPA in 1980.[7] At the time there were twelve ZAC's in Saint-Quentin-en-Yvelines (see figure 3–1). The statement was created by combining the flows of expenses and receipts for each of these twelve ZAC's. The 1980 date is arbitrary because most of them will still be in the process of development at that time (see table 3–3). In addition, new ZAC's may be initiated in the late 1970s that are not reflected in the calculations.

Through 1975 the twelve projects had accumulated 363 million francs in expenses that had to be counted in the EPA's balance sheet (excluding government grants). These expenses included 124 million francs for land acquisition, 103 million for utilities, 21 million for studies and publicity, 36 million for salaries, 16 million in interest payments on loans, and 74 million in other expenses. Land sales had brought in 149 million francs and other fees and special grants 78 million. The EPA had borrowed 169 million francs, of which 23 million had been repaid, leaving a net debt of 146 million francs.

By 1980, the deficit is expected to be reduced to 52 million francs, based on a detailed study of each ZAC under development. Only one of the ZAC's, Elancourt-Maurepas, is expected to show a positive balance by 1980. There are two reasons for deficits in the other ZAC's. First, the expenses for land acquisition and site preparation will have been incurred before 1980, but not all the improved sites will

---

[7]Etablissement Public d'Aménagement de la Ville Nouvelle de Saint-Quentin-en-Yvelines, "Plan financier à l'horizon 1980 de l'établissement Public de la ville nouvelle de Saint-Quentin-en-Yvelines," mimeographed (Saint-Quentin-en-Yvelines: Etablissement Public d'Aménagement de la Ville Nouvelle de Saint-Quentin-en-Yvelines, 1974).

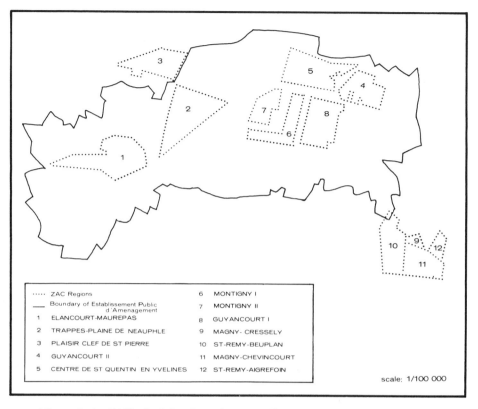

Figure 3–1. ZAC's in Saint-Quentin-en-Yvelines. The new town is divided into Zones d'Aménagement Concerté, where new development is concentrated. Each ZAC has its own long-term financing plan.

have been sold to private developers. Second, the so-called indirect costs of development exceed anticipated receipts. Land sales and other direct receipts are expected to bring in 710 million francs by 1980, while expenses for land acquisition, site preparation, and studies will amount to only 621 million, a positive balance of 89 million francs. However, the expenses of salaries and special efforts to assist the development process, such as the construction of temporary homes for construction workers, are expected to amount to 136 million francs more than the receipts generated from these projects. Payment of interest charges will account for another 46 million francs, bringing the deficit for the twelve projects to 93 million. The net deficit is reduced to 52 million francs because a profit of 42 million is anticipated on a variety of special projects built and operated by the EPA, which can not be attributed to particular ZAC's (see table 3–4).

Table 3–3. Construction in Progress for the Saint-Quentin-en-Yvelines EPA

Type of Construction	1975 Total	Projected Figures for 1980								
		Total	ZAC's*							
			1	2	3	4	5	6–8	9–12	
Commercial (m^2)	34,700	70,200	9,000	7,500	6,600	3,500	21,600	14,000	8,000	
Housing (dwelling units)	10,310	42,210	6,600	4,000	5,300	1,960	8,200	12,400	3,750	
Industry (hectares)	7.8	98.5	4.8	22.5		14.2		45.0	12.0	
Offices (m^2)	133,000	672,000	22,000	10,000			640,000			

*ZAC's: (1) Elancourt–Maurepas; (2) Trappes–Plaine de Neauphle; (3) Plaisir–Clef de Saint-Pierre; (4) Guyancourt II; (5) Centre de Saint-Quentin-en-Yvelines; (6) Montigny I; (7) Montigny II; (8) Guyancourt I; (9) Magny-les-Hameaux–Cressely; (10) Saint-Remy-les-Chevreuse–Beauplan; (11) Magny-les-Hameaux–Chevincourt; (12) Saint-Remy-les-Chevreuse–Aigrefoin. The location of the twelve ZAC's within Saint-Quentin-en-Yvelines can be seen in figure 3–1.

Table 3-4. Financial Statement for the Saint-Quentin-en-Yvelines EPA (in millions of francs)

Item	1975 Total	Projected Figures for 1980							
		ZAC's*							
		Total	1	2	3	4	5	6–8	9–12
Direct receipts									
Land sales									
Commercial	9	17	1	3	1	1	7	2	2
Housing	99	455	90	41	59	26	115	78	46
Industrial	8	70	3	22		10		24	11
Offices	33	85	5	1			79		
Other	9	82	31	3	3	4	30	6	5
Total direct receipts	158	709	130	70	63	41	231	110	64
Direct expenses									
Land acquisition	124	176	20	15	17	11	24	64	25
Infrastructure	103	371	38	48	33	18	141	58	35
Studies	21	35	5	4	3	1	11	8	3
Other	74	39	20				19		
Total direct expenses	322	621	83	67	53	30	195	130	63
Net direct receipts/expenses	-164	88	47	3	10	11	36	-20	1
Indirect receipts/expenses	34	-135	-22	-13	-13	-12	-38	-25	-12
Interest expenses	16	46	6	5	4	2	14	10	5
Net receipts/expenses	-146	-93	19	-15	-7	-3	-16	-55	-16

NOTE: This table shows the predicted cumulative profit or loss in 1980 for the twelve ZAC's under way in Saint-Quentin-en-Yvelines as of 1975. All but one are expected to show a net deficit. These deficits can be traced to two causes. First, virtually all the direct expenses for land acquisition and infrastructure will be paid by 1980, but not all the prepared land will have been sold to developers. The balance between direct expenses and receipts will be more positive in the longer term. Second, the projects incur heavy indirect expenses, such as salaries, publicity, and the construction of temporary housing for construction workers.

*ZAC's: (1) Elancourt–Maurepas; (2) Trappes–Plaine de Neauphle; (3) Plaisir–Clef de Saint-Pierre; (4) Guyancourt II; (5) Centre de Saint-Quentin-en-Yvelines; (6) Montigny I; (7) Montigny II; (8) Guyancourt I; (9) Magny-les-Hameaux–Cressely; (10) Saint-Remy-les-Chevreuse–Beauplan; (11) Magny-les-Hameaux–Chevincourt; (12) Saint-Remy-les-Chevreuse–Aigrefoin. The location of the twelve ZAC's within Saint-Quentin-en-Yvelines can be seen in figure 3–1.

COMPARATIVE COSTS OF NEW TOWNS AND ALTERNATIVE PROJECTS

Because of the lack of systematic data concerning the financial prospects of the new towns it is not yet totally possible to compare them with more conventional projects. The Groupe Central des Villes Nouvelles has argued that the new towns are cheaper than other forms of urban development in France. While admitting that objective evidence is not readily available, the GCVN argued that new towns are falsely judged more expensive because of their prominence. Furthermore, because they attempt to include all the costs of urban development, new towns do not have surprise unexpected costs as do traditional projects.

In an era of rapid urban growth, as experienced in France today, large-scale new projects are required to provide the expanding urban population with many services and facilities. Consequently, urban development projects are needed on a larger scale, covering thirty years instead of ten, several thousand hectares instead of several dozen, and hundreds of thousands of new residents instead of tens of thousands. The large-scale increase in demand for services and facilities cannot be met by a marginal increase in the use of existing public equipment because that is already overloaded. According to the GCVN:

> This change of dimension in the order of needs has a major consequence, namely, that the marginal utilization of existing equipment is no longer possible, not only because of the accumulated delays in the revitalization of normal equipment, which should have accompanied urbanization in recent years, but also because of the increase in demand. New infrastructure is thus required to welcome hundreds of thousands of houses and jobs in the large urban areas. [8]

Even without a large population increase, additional equipment is necessary to serve the existing population. The new towns attempt to concentrate the new services and facilities required for the expanding population. These services and facilities, which will be needed in any event, can be more economically provided by new towns for three reasons: (1) the land is acquired at lower prices; (2) the building of infrastructure in new towns is cheaper than adding the same level of services to already built-up areas; and (3) the new towns are located at transport nodes, to take advantage of underused interurban

---

[8]Groupe Central des Villes Nouvelles, "Note sur le côut de réalisation des villes nouvelles," mimeographed (Paris: Groupe Centrale des Villes Nouvelles), pp. 1–2, my translation.

expressways and rail lines. There is no difference between building superstructures in a new town or anywhere else. The bricks and mortar for school buildings, social centers, and clinics cost the same everywhere. The difference in cost between new towns and other sites is due entirely to land acquisition and the installation of infrastructure.

Local officials believe that the new towns will swallow up a large percentage of the budget for infrastructure in the department or region. The GCVN points out that this fear is irrational; if new towns weren't being built other local authorities might have more money for infrastructure but also many more new residents to accommodate. Nonetheless, the system of isolating the national grants for new towns does make them a convenient target for attack by local authorities.

In order to compare the costs of development of new towns with more traditional projects, the GCVN compared the cost per dwelling of land acquisition and utilities for new towns and projects in the inner suburbs and in other outer suburbs of Paris. Land for the new towns was much cheaper — 2,200 francs per dwelling, compared to 13,500 in the inner suburbs and 4,800 in the outer. The cost of tertiary equipment (direct utility connections to the individual dwellings) was estimated at 4,800 for the inner suburbs and 6,600 for the outer. These figures were compared with 10,000 francs per dwelling for both secondary and tertiary equipment in the new towns (table 3–5). The rationale for comparing the cost of secondary and tertiary equipment in the new towns with just tertiary elsewhere is that in the traditional suburbs new projects often hook into existing water and sewer systems. On this basis, land and eqipment costs 11,400 francs per dwelling in the outer suburbs, 12,200 in the new towns, and 18,100 in the inner suburbs. Even with the higher utility costs the new towns

Table 3–5. Comparative Costs of Construction of Infrastructure and Land Acquisition at Various Locations in the Paris Region (in francs per dwelling unit)*

Location	Land	Secondary Equipment	Tertiary Equipment	Total Cost
Inner suburbs	13,500	3,000	4,600	21,800
Outer suburbs	4,800	3,700	6,600	15,100
New towns	2,200	10,000		12,200

* These figures are based on estimates developed by the Groupe Central des Villes Nouvelles.

are still competitive with projects in the outer suburbs and they are cheaper than the inner suburbs.[9]

Other studies indicate that the cost of land is so high in the Paris region that the savings on land acquisition in the new towns more than offsets the additional infrastructure expenses. Land has averaged about 75,000 francs per hectare in the Paris new towns and 55,000 for the provinces (about $7,000 and $5,000 per acre, respectively, at current exchange rates). The land costs have varied from a low of about 36,000 francs per hectare ($3,500 per acre) at L'Isle d'Abeau and 44,000 francs per hectare ($4,000 per acre) at Melun-Sénart to a high of 105,000 francs per hectare ($10,000 per acre) at Lille-Est and 132,000 francs per hectare ($13,000 per acre) at Cergy-Pontoise. While these figures seem high in comparison with other countries, it must be pointed out that land acquisition costs are quite high, especially in the Paris region. Land for new towns is being bought at prices five to ten times lower than comparable sites elsewhere in the outer suburbs and over one hundred times lower than the inner suburbs and central Paris. Two large redevelopment schemes inside the continuously built-up area are La Défense, just to the west of central Paris, and Front-de-Seine, on railroad land along the left bank of the Seine near the Eiffel Tower. The cost per acre of land at La Défense was over one million dollars while the land at Front-de-Seine cost about 1.6 million dollars per acre.

The rationale for building new towns is partly due to the fact that existing equipment is already overloaded. It can be argued that large-scale construction further in would require new secondary and tertiary equipment to accommodate the large population increase.. If land acquisition and secondary and tertiary equipment costs are compared at each location, the new towns would run 12,200 francs per dwelling unit, the outer suburbs 15,100, and the inner suburbs 21,800.

A second study by the GCVN compares the total costs of new infrastructure per new inhabitant in new towns of Evry and Cergy-Pontoise and the cities of Orléans, Rennes, and Tours. The study found that in the existing towns 1,633 francs per new inhabitant was spent on new infrastructure, compared to 975 francs per new inhabitant in the new towns. In the Rouen region for the period of

---

[9] Groupe Central des Villes Nouvelles, "Eléments généraux et examples du côut comparé d l'urbanisation en villes nouvelles et de l'urbanisation par développement des métropoles," mimeographed (Paris: Groupe Centrale des Villes Nouvelles, 1970), p.1.

1960–67, 350 million francs was spent on new infrastructure and 155 million for land acquisition, while the population increased 41,500. In 1970 francs, the expenditure was 2,500 francs per new inhabitant. At Le Vaudreuil, outside of Rouen, 52 million francs was spent for 6,500 new inhabitants, or 1,600 per new inhabitant. [10]

A third study by the GCVN compared the cost of growth in the Lyon region and its new town of L'Isle d'Abeau. In L'Isle d'Abeau between 1968 and 1972, 6,500 dwellings were started, around 14.7 percent of the total for the Lyon region. In addition, 200 hectares of industrial land was developed, one-third of the regional total. Expenditures in the Lyon region as a whole included 329 million francs for roads, 91 million for sewers and 192 million for water systems, making a total of 641.0 million francs. At L'Isle d'Abeau expenditures included 20 million francs for roads, 9.5 million for sewers, 5.25 million for water, and 3.5 million for garbage disposal, a total of 28.25 million francs, or 6 percent of the regional expenditures. Thus, for 14.7 percent of the housing starts and 33 percent of the industrial zone developments, the infrastructure costs for L'Isle d'Abeau were 6 percent of those of the Lyon region. [11]

If projects of the same density are compared for different locations in France, the new towns appear to be competitive with other projects. Land costs much less per hectare at new town locations than elsewhere in the Paris region, as much as five hundred times cheaper, while utility costs are not that much higher.

In reality, comparisons become much more complex than the French evidence has revealed. However, no comprehensive model has been created to compare systematically the construction costs of new towns and alternative forms of urban development. One American study, *The Costs of Sprawl*, has given a partial answer. Prepared by the Real Estate Research Corporation for the Council on Environmental Quality, the Department of Housing and Urban Development, and the Environmental Protection Agency, the 1974 study compared the costs of development for a variety of typical projects on the periphery of urban areas. [12] *The Costs of Sprawl* identified six different projects, each with 10,000 dwellings on a 6,000-acre tract (comparable to the size of smaller new towns). The six projects were designed to compare planned development as opposed to sprawl, and high net residential density as opposed to low density.

[10] Ibid., p.3.
[11] Ibid., pp. 4–5.
[12] Real Estate Research Corporation, *The Costs of Sprawl* (Washington, D.C.: Government Printing Office, 1974).

Planned Development vs. Sprawl

To understand the impact of sprawl on development costs, *The Costs of Sprawl* compared three typical projects: planned mix communities, combination mix communities, and sprawl mix communities.

The three projects had the same mix of housing styles, net residential density, and total project acreage. The difference among the three came from the pattern of development within the 6,ooo-acre sites. The planned mix community had all development contiguous, leaving large areas of public open space. The sprawl mix community was organized in the typical suburban manner, with discontinuous development spread out over the entire 6,000-acre site, and little community open space. The combination mix community contained half typical sprawl and half planned contiguous development.

The study then compared the capital and operating costs of the three alternatives (see table 3–6). The capital cost of the planned mix development was $357.5 million, compared to 368.2 million for the combination mix and $372.8 million for the sprawl mix alternative. The planned mix had higher costs for open space and recreation development but major savings for utilities. Open space cost $3 million in the planned mix alternative, 11 percent higher than for spawl mix. The additional expenditure of $300,000 for open space was more than offset by significant savings in the costly utility bills. Roads cost $27.1 million in the planned mix, compared to $32.4 in the sprawl mix; utilities $33.2 million in the planned mix, compared to $38.7 million in the sprawl mix, for an overall savings of $10.8 million for infrastructure in the planned mix alternative. Operating and maintenance costs were virtually identical for the three alternatives. Ten-year operating costs were estimated at $19.4 million for planned mix, $19.5 for combination mix, and $19.7 million for sprawl mix.

High Density vs. Low Density

The second set of comparisons attempted to demonstrate the impact of higher net residential density. The study therefore examined examples of projects with different mixes of housing styles. Four alternatives were considered, including the planned mix community already discussed. Planned mix contained 20 percent each of five different housing styles: conventional single-family dwellings on half-acre tracts, clustered single-family dwellings on 0.4-acre tracts, clustered townhouses on 0.3-acre lots, walk-up apartments, five units

Table 3–6. The Costs of Sprawl Community Cost Analysis (in thousands of dollars)

Cost Category	Planned Mix		Combination Mix		Sprawl Mix		Low Density Planned		Low Density Sprawl		High Density Planned	
	Capital Cost	Operating Cost	Capital Cost	Operating Cost	Capital Cost	Operating Cost	Capital Cost	Operating Cost	Capital Cost	Operating Cost	Capital Cost	Operating Cost
Open space/recreation	2,968	380	2,862	320	2,684	260	2,968	380	2,684	260	2,968	380
Schools	45,382	9,643	45,382	9,652	45,382	9,737	45,382	9,643	45,382	9,737	45,382	9,643
Public facilities	16,216	5,103	16,441	5,296	16,453	5,405	16,259	5,165	16,615	5,575	16,304	5,164
Transport	27,077	260	29,768	260	32,353	261	33,770	354	37,965	396	22,862	209
Utilities	33,227	3,987	36,042	3,988	38,684	3,989	47,444	5,130	61,974	5,141	22,432	3,335
Residential	214,172		214,172		214,172		318,291		320,400		160,300	
Land	18,491		23,531		23,105		25,692		29,539		16,814	
Total	357,533	19,373	368,162	19,516	372,833	19,652	489,806	20,672	514,559	21,109	287,062	18,731

SOURCE: Real Estate Research Corporation. *The Costs of Sprawl* (Washington, D.C.: Government Printing Office, 1974), pp. 9–11.

NOTE: The six alternatives created by *The Costs of Sprawl* study were designed to compare the costs of construction and operations over ten years for different patterns of housing. The study demonstrated that high density planned communities would cost less than lower density planned communities and much less than unplanned sprawl.

to the acre, and high-rise apartments, ten units to the acre. The low density planned community contained 75 percent clustered single-family dwellings and 25 percent conventional single-family houses. The low density sprawl contained 75 percent conventional single-family dwellings and 25 percent clustered. The high density planned alternative contained 10 percent single-family clustered, 20 percent townhouses, 30 percent walk-up apartments, and 40 percent high-rise apartments. As a result of these differences, the amount of land within the 6,000-acre site devoted to residential use ranged from 733 acres for the high density community to 1,450 acres for the planned mix communtiy, 2,333 acres for the low density planned community, and 3,600 acres for low density sprawl.

According to *The Costs of Sprawl*, the high density planned communtiy is significantly cheaper than the other alternatives. The capital cost of high density planned community was $287.1 million, compared to $357.5 million for the planned mix, $489.8 million for the low density planned, and $514.6 million for the low density sprawl. Significant cost savings for the high density alternative came from utilities, roads, and housing. The low density planned community required expenditures of $33.9 million for roads and $47.4 million for utilities, compared to $22.9 million and $22.4 million for these two categories in the high density planned community. Infrastructure was much cheaper in the high density alternative primarily because more of the site could be left unimproved since development was concentrated on a relatively small portion of the site. Housing construction costs were $160.3 million in the high density alternative and $318.3 in the low density. Ten-year operating and maintenance costs were $18.7 million in the high density planned community, compared to $19.4 million for the planned mix community, $20.7 million for low density planned, and $21.1 million for low density sprawl.

The Costs of Sprawl concluded that planned developments can offer significant cost savings over unplanned sprawl, primarily through more efficient provision of infrastructure. However, more significant saving are registered when development is concentrated into higher net residential density, again because much of the site can be left unimproved. A high density planned community, containing about half apartments, is only around half the cost of an unplanned, predominantly single-family project.

For new towns advocates the major deficiency of *The Costs of Sprawl* study was the decision to hold land acquisition costs constant. All alternatives were assumed to be built on peripheral sites where land acquisition costs were relatively low. The only difference in land acquisition costs among the six alternatives derived from the fact that the planned high density and mixed alternatives required less land for housing and could therefore leave more unimproved land in the site unacquired. *The Costs of Sprawl* estimated land acquisition costs at $16.8 million for the high density planned and $18.5 million for the planned mix alternative. The unplanned low density alternative was $29.5 million. Thus, land acquisition costs for all six alternatives were in the range of $5,000 to $6,000 per acre.

Because of their peripheral location land is much cheaper in new towns than elsewhere in the urban region. Land costs on the periphery, where a new town would be constructed are about $5,000 per acre. In the built-up suburbs it is approximately $50,000 per acre, and in the central city it is about $500,000 per acre, although the figures presented above for Paris are even higher. New towns supporters argue that the major savings in land acquisition costs offset any additional utility or transportation expenditures. A 6,000-acre tract costs around $30 million in the periphery. If it is assumed that only 1,000 acres is needed in the built-up area for the construction of high rises, the land acquisition costs will still vary between $300 million and $3 billion, a figure that overwhelms any marginal savings in utility and transportation costs in the built-up area.

New towns advocates support *The Costs of Sprawl* conclusion concerning the comparison between sprawl and a planned mixed development. However, the study does not cover the most significant cost variable in the urban area, the difference in land acquisition costs, which is the foundation of the economic rationale for planned peripheral development as opposed to central redevelopment at high densities.

Despite the evidence that new towns may be more profitable in the long run than alternative forms of urban development, they still remain impractical economic ventures. The fact that new towns may be economically attractive from an overall view is beside the point in a free market economy. New towns cannot be built at a profit by private developers, while alternatives can. The reason is that new towns are too large for a private developer to manage. The nine French new towns have already spent about three billion francs. Although by the 1980s the new towns may well show a substantial profit, no private developer can tie up three billion francs for fifteen years. Only the national government has the resources to make investments and accept profits over the long-term period and large scale of operation required for new towns. The realization that new towns are too big for private developers does not mean that the private sector must necessarily be eliminated from the new towns development process. As will be shown in the next chapter, the French government has reserved a large role for private developers in the new towns, but it takes the lead when the private sector can't cope.

4

THE ROLE
OF THE PRIVATE SECTOR

France has a fundamentally liberal economy. The cooperation of the private sector has therefore proven indispensible to the construction of new towns. The relatively limited powers exercised by the EPA planners, in contrast to those of the British-style development corporation, illustrate the orientation of the French planning system. Without the involvement of private builders and developers the new towns plans could never be transformed into reality. The development process has of necessity been designed to achieve a division of responsibility among the national planners, the local authorities, and the private sector that secures both private profits and public control over the location of new development.

In Great Britain the public sector performs virtually all the tasks associated with building of the new towns, while the American new towns are almost entirely private ventures. The American experience has demonstrated conclusively that private enterprise cannot successfully build new towns without public financial support. The French new towns program is extremely important for American planners because it has provided a rational division of responsibilities between the public and private sectors.

In a basically liberal economy private developers must be lured to the new towns. The French planners try to guide private development to the new towns and away from undesired locations with a combination of inducements and controls. They have concluded that the key to inducing developers to the new towns is encouraging them to operate at their accustomed scale. New towns are distinguished from more traditional projects by the scale of operations. Whereas a typical development might borrow $10 million for five years to build five hundred dwellings, a new town required a loan of $200 million for twenty years for one hundred thousand dwellings. This scale is too large for private developers. The publicly sponsored Etablissement Public d'Aménagement therefore plays the role of prime developer. It buys the large new town site, installs needed infrastructure, and sells the land in small units to private developers. French developers, relatively large and efficient by international standards, make a profit primarily by the construction and management of buildings rather than by land speculation. Private developers buy or lease land from the EPA, complete the preparations on it, arrange the financing for the buildings, and construct them. They build and/or operate housing, offices, shops, and industries in the new towns. Although many French developers are capable of building several hundred housing units a year, none is big enough to manage an entire new town. Only the government has the resources to assume the financial risks and uncertainties of a project that size.

The new towns have been created in an atmosphere of cooperation between the public and private sectors. This is consistent with the overall orientation of public policy in the Fifth Republic, which has been dominated by de Gaulle and his party. Neither national nor local government officials—at least those in power—view the private sector with hostility. At a personal level there is a considerable amount of movement between the private and public sectors. Public and private officials are trained at the same group of elite schools. In the urban development field, the private developer may be a classmate of the government official who has to approve the plan or issue a permit. A high degree of informal cooperation is thus inevitable. Public officials may be searching for more lucrative private sector positions. Such an official can demonstrate his value to a private developer by expediting the process of approval for a project. In return the official could subsequently receive a high-paying job in the private sector.

Institutionally, the distinction between the private and public sectors in France is not very clear. Since World War II a number of industries have been nationalized, but their management policies are indistinguishable from private firms. Other firms have not been fully nationalized but the government has the right to appoint a percentage of the board of directors. Still others are privately managed but survive only with government subsidies. Throughout the economy, monopolization and interlocking directorates have been encouraged to a much higher degree than in other western societies. Therefore, when reference is made to private-sector activities in France, the observer must always be aware that at least indirect public involvement is still likely.

As was the case with the relations between local authorities and the government, the theoretical division of powers does not reflect the true relationships. In theory, the national government and local officials have a good deal of power over private developers. Local governments issue building permits, operate planning and zoning controls, and provide infrastructure. The national government provides subsidies to local officials and private developers and approves local planning proposals. However, in reality large private developers have considerable power, especially over the local authorities, who can be persuaded by skilled businessmen to issue the needed permits. The most important tool available to the private sector, though, is the power of the market. As in the United States, the imposition of planning controls must balance the desires of the private sector to build where the market appears strongest with the public interest concerning the best locations to build. If government officials do not permit construction where consumers and developers demand it, a good deal of opposition could be generated, and needed new projects would not be built. The controls can bend the market but they cannot successfully break it.

To understand the role of the private sector in the new towns development process, it is necessary to recognize that private developers are concerned with two basic issues: What is the market for new housing or nonresidential facilities, and where is land available for development? The answer to the first question is less conducive to the development of new towns than the second.

THE PRIVATE SECTOR VIEW

If market forces were permitted to operate without government influence, new towns would never be built. Part of the problem is that many of the services and facilities essential for a new town are unprofitable for the private sector to provide without government assistance. Among these components are recreational facilities, low-income housing, and new schools. This problem can be overcome with selective governmental intervention and subsidies.

The fundamental obstacle to private development of new towns is the absence of a strong market for the product. Private participation in new towns is useless if the housing and nonresidential functions in the project can't be sold or rented to firms and individuals at a profitable price. New towns must therefore be located where the potential market demand is great enough to encourage private sector involvement. The dilemma for the French new towns is clear: if they were located where the market was sufficiently strong, then massive public intervention would not be needed. If they were located where no market demands were present, then the private sector would be unwilling to participate in their development. The program represents the extreme to which the market can be bent while still retaining private sector involvement. In fact, at some of the new towns the delicate balance has not been achieved: in some cases private developers are clamoring for participation while in others they are scarce. The differences in achievement among the new towns in the long run are based on how sympathetic each is to the market pressures.

France today is a booming country for private developers. Part of the demand for new housing is due to factors common to other western countries, such as the trend to smaller households, higher average incomes, and the replacement of old substandard units. The boom is particularly strong in France because of the relatively rapid population increase and the failure to eliminate fully the wartime shortages.

The most dynamic housing market in France is in the Paris region. Despite national government efforts to restrict its growth, the region today adds just over 100,000 dwelling units per year. Many officials, especially in the DATAR, consider this figure too high. They argue that fewer permits should be granted by the local authorities and fewer housing subsidies made available by the government for low-income housing. On the other hand many developers feel that they cannot satisfy the market demand for housing in the Paris region within the 100,000-unit limitation.

In view of the difficulties in efficiently and effectively imposing limits on agreements between communes and developers constructing unassisted housing, any reduction in the number of new housing units in the Paris region is certain to affect the low- and moderate-cost markets. Because of the shortage of low-cost housing in the Paris region, planners are reluctant to curtail further the assisted housing starts. The 100,000-unit figure has therefore become a widely accepted compromise though it is an arbitrary limitation.

About 45 percent of the housing starts are to accommodate the natural population increase in the Paris region, that is, the excess of births and immigrants over deaths and emigrants. About 40 percent are for the replacement of substandard and demolished units, while 15 percent are to accommodate the trend toward smaller households.[1]

[1]Préfecture de la Région Parisienne, *La Région parisienne: 4 années d'aménagement et d'équipement, 1969–1972* (Paris: Préfecture de la Région Parisienne, 1973), p. 62.

The 100,000 annual housing starts are not distributed randomly in the Paris region. Paris consists of a number of submarkets—at least thirty according to a 1970 analysis.[2] Each of these has distinctive characteristics. An understanding of the problems associated with private sector involvement in the new towns development process must be based on an examination of the relationship between the new towns and the various submarkets of the Paris region. The construction attracted to the new towns will be shaped by the character of the submarkets within which the towns are located.

From the viewpoint of private developers considering investment in the new towns, the most significant fact is their peripheral location. Between 1949 and 1965, when the new towns were proposed, about 633,000 housing units had been built in the Paris region: 115,000 units were built in central Paris, 178,000 up to 10 kilometers from the center, and 111,900 between 10 and 12.4 kilometers away. Thus, over 400,000, or just under two-thirds of the new housing units in the region, were located within 12.5 kilometers of the center. There were about 122,600 (about 20 percent) added between 12.5 and 24.9 kilometers from the center, leaving only 33,500 (5 percent) beyond 25 kilometers. Marne-la-Vallée is located 10 kilometers from central Paris, Evry and Cergy-Pontoise 25 kilometers away, Saint-Quentin-en-Yvelines 30 kilometers away, and Melun-Sénart 35 kilometers away.

The percentage of housing starts beyond 25 kilometers increased from 5 to 10 percent in the late 1960s. If this trend continues, the market for housing beyond 25 kilometers could increase to 20,000 units per year (a 20-percent increase) by the late 1970s. The central Paris housing market has stabilized at around 10,000 units per year, so that any increase beyond 25 kilometers would reduce construction in inner suburbs. In the early 1970s, about 10 percent of the 10,000 units beyond 25 kilometers comprised single-family and second homes. The remainder was divided equally between private and publicly assisted apartment complexes. Thus, in 1970 about 4,500 units built beyond 25 kilometers were publicly assisted apartments, with 9,000 forecast by the late 1970s, given existing market trends.[3]

The five new towns are planned to welcome about 15,000 new publicly assisted units per year. About 10,000 other subsidized units per year have been programmed at other locations approved prior to the new towns, for a total of 25,000 publicly assisted units per year

[2]Charles Julienne, "La Segmentation du marché immobilier dans la région parisienne" (Paper from IRCOM seminar, 1970).
[3]Ibid., pp. 4–5.

planned in the outer suburbs. However, according to market trends, only 9,000 publicly assisted units are projected beyond 25 kilometers from central Paris. The construction of 15,000 units per year in the new towns is thus impossible unless prevailing market conditions are sharply altered. Because a significant increase in the total number of annual housing starts permitted in the Paris region is unlikely, three policy alternatives are available to bring the new town goals in line with market realities. First, the number of new units built in peripheral locations other than new towns could be sharply reduced. This alternative is unrealistic in view of current commitments outside the new towns. The second option would be simply to reduce the goals of the new towns. As will be seen, this strategy has been used in part. The third alternative is to make the new town market more attractive than the inner suburbs for consumers and developers. This effort, favored by most planners, requires two actions: the discourage-ment of new construction in the inner suburbs and locations other than new towns (discussed in this chapter), and the creation of a higher-quality product in the new towns than elsewhere (discussed in Chapter 5).

The second issue facing private developers is the availability of land for new projects. Unlike the issue of predominant market trends, the problem of land availability has been conducive to the establish-ment of a national urban growth policy that includes the new towns. At first glance there does not appear to be a land availability problem in France, particularly in comparison to other European neighbors. Of the 55 million hectares in France, only around 3 percent is urbanized, more comparable to the situation in the United States than other European countries. Agricultural activity uses 34 million hec-tares, while forests cover another 12 million hectares.[4] Current demand for additional urban land is around 15,000 hectares per year.

In the late 1960s government planners and private developers debated the reasons for the lack of availability of land for urban development. One group of officials argued that the problem was due to government controls. Their chief spokesman was Albin Chalandon, who became the minister of equipment after the upheavals of 1968, during the period when the new towns program was moving from the planning to the construction stage. The criticism was directed at a number of new national programs developed in the late 1950s and early 1960s, including the new towns, but the chief target was the right of local authorities to grant building permits. The Chalandon

[4]Philippe Pinchemel, *France: A Geographical Survey* (New York and Washington, D.C.: Praeger, 1969), p. 261.

view was that the planning tools had caused more problems than they had solved. The lack of land was due to the refusal by communal officials to issue more building permits and to the insistence by national officials that private developers build in a few locations such as new towns. The result of these controls was an increase in land prices for the relatively few areas where development permission was granted. To the planners, if 15,000 hectares of land were needed each year for new urban development, then it was the job of the planners to provide those 15,000 hectares. The proper amount of new land should be identified and selected, equipped with needed services, frozen in price, and disposed of to the appropriate developers.

This argument was opposed by Chalandon and other "free marketers" because the system failed to stifle the rise in land prices adequately, especially in the Paris region. Chalandon claimed that a more efficient method of keeping down the land prices would be to abolish the system of planning control and open up more land for development. The local building permit system should be eliminated and the master plans at the regional and local levels modified to permit construction over more areas of the region. Land that in the public interest should be protected from development, such as forests and areas of scenic beauty, should be acquired by the state. But land with no explicit public welfare rationale for being withheld from potential development should be freed of restrictions and made available for developers. In this way developers would be able to choose to build where the market, not the planner, dictated. The final product would be cheaper than that currently offered because the supply of land available for development would exceed the demand; the monopoly value attached to developable land in a scarcity situation would be eliminated. Therefore, two or three times the land required for urban development should be made available to builders.

New towns were considered an untried tool that carried an unacceptable risk. Given the administrative and economic difficulties with the new towns it was dangerous to place too much reliance on large-scale planned growth in a few locations. As Chalandon put it,

> When I came to the equipment ministry I was struck by the discrepancy between the decision to build eight or nine new towns and the financial possibilities. I was also struck by the risk that was taken in building so many towns without any previous experience. I thought it would be much better to try one or two to see if they succeeded—to see if our people got used to them—and if the results were good, to go ahead. If nothing had been done before my coming to the ministry, I would have built some, but there were nine new towns not really under construction but approved in committees. I made the decision to reduce the number of new towns; just five were taken into consideration, the ones now under construction. My

postition was that a balance had to found between development through new towns and development through old towns.[5]

Instead of building only new towns, Chalandon advocated development of a large number of small projects that he called "villages," to be built outside of existing middle-sized towns beyond the fringe of the Paris region. His strategy was to work with towns about 100 kilometers from Paris (three times the distance of the new towns) with populations of about 100,000. These towns could be expanded by constructing large "villages" on their perimeter. Because villages would be located far from central Paris most residents could live in single-family houses rather than apartment buildings, which were required in the small, high-priced tracts of land closer to Paris. Chalandon cited the desires of most French families (like those in other countries) to live in single-family houses. While he was in office, Chalandon sponsored several competitions for the design of these villages.

The fatal flaw in Chalandon's argument was that the problem is not the lack of land per se, but the lack of developable land. The construction of new residential or nonresidential structures can only be carried out if supporting infrastructure is available, such as roads, gas, electricity, running water, and sewerage systems. The shortage of land equipped with the needed infrastructure is due entirely to the method of supplying it in France. The provision of infrastructure is primarily a local government responsibility. As I have said, most local authorities are financially incapable of meeting large-scale demands for new services without state aid; even with government intervention, finances are shaky. Unless public financing of new utilities continued, the supply of developable land in France would shrink further. A developer could not be expected to undertake the cost of putting in infrastructure himself; if he did, he would have to charge higher prices for his homes than a developer building on equipped land. In the long run the problem could be overcome: if no equipped land at all were available, then developers would have to install their own services. But to reach that position would be politically and socially unacceptable, because it would involve many years of extremely high land and housing costs. Therefore, the government had to continue its policy of intervention in the housing market through the provision of supporting utilities and services. Given that reality, two policies are possible. The first is to equip and service two or three times the amount of land needed for urban development. This strategy would glut the housing market with an oversupply of land and would keep prices down. Although it would be interesting to see

[5]Interview with Albin Chalandon, July 1974.

whether or not the total cost of such oversupply of facilities would offset the lower land costs, from the government point of view this strategy would involve a very high level of expenditure to provide the facilities. The more politically and financially practical strategy was to continue the policy of equipping just as much land as was needed for development and to negotiate with the developers over the division of responsibility for the payment of the improvements. But this strategy therefore required governmental location decisions on which sites would be equipped. Because of the need for government involvement in the urban development process through the support for infrastructure investment, the Chalandon view was rejected. The debate instead concerned the appropriate policies and tools to be adopted.

The creation of new towns with private sector involvement thus has required a delicate balancing of conflicting development pressures. In support of the concentration of new growth in new towns is the shortage of land equipped with the needed infrastructure. On the other hand, market forces are demanding other locations for new projects. The task for government planners who favor the new towns policy has been to fashion administrative tools to guide private development toward the new towns. If the planners are too heavy-handed the private sector will simply not participate in their realization. If private developers are given too much leeway, they will not choose to build in new towns. The public sector has a trump card to play in this process: because the government controls the location of new infrastructure the private sector is limited in where new projects can be located. The planners have attempted to use this strength to influence private sector location decisions to a greater extent than would otherwise be possible.

PLANNING TOOLS

There are three sets of tools by which the French government attempts to channel urban growth into towns and other preferred areas: (1) the creation of planning and zoning regulations; (2) controlling the ownership and price of land needed for urban development; (3) a formal mechanism for subdividing the large new town site into smaller units manageable by private developers.

Creation of Master Plans and Zoning: SDAU's and POS's

The creation of master plans involves two problems. First, how do you ensure that national and regional plans are carried over into consistent local plans; and second, how do you make sure that the local plans are effective? The French have created a system of local master plans approved by national planners. The 1967 law of orientation for land development[6] requires the creation of local master plans, called the Schéma Directeur d'Aménagement et d'Urbanisme (SDAU). This plan established the broad development patterns for a commune or group of communes particularly affected by urban growth. It also indicates new public works that are planned for the area, though not their precise location. The SDAU is ''not so much a long-run forecast as a context or framework for the critical examination of decisions. The drawing up of the SDAU first brings to light the main foreseeable difficulties that will be encountered and proposes a certain number of at least partial remedies. It also defines various 'negative options,' such as open spaces to be excluded from all future urbanization. In other words, it should result in the establishment of the — often narrow — limits within which real choices are still possible.''[7]

The master plans include a written report and maps. The report contains an analysis of the existing situation in the area, the strategy of development adopted, with justification, and an indication of the time frame of development. The graphic presentation includes: (a) the general direction of growth; (b) the important open spaces to be maintained or created; (c) the major urban and natural areas to be protected; (d) the location of principal industries and the most important infrastructure of public interest; (3) the general organization of transportation and plans for future construction; (f) the essential water, sewage, and waste treatment systems; and (g) the districts requiring more detailed study.

Master plans have been developed for each of the new towns by the EPA or its predecessor, the MEA. In the new towns with more than one SCA, one master plan has been made for each. The new town master plans must be approved by the SCA, the regional prefect, and the relevant ministries. Master plans developed outside the new towns are governed by a more complex set of rules. The regional prefect (specifically the regional representative of the minister of equipment, the SRE) establishes the territory to be covered by the plan and issues directives to be followed in the preparation of it. These directives establish the future population targets for the area covered by the master plan. They also inform the local planners about new projects being built by the region or state that must be located within the study area. Examples of these constraints include expressways, universities, and national parks.

6
The Loi d'Orientation Fonciere (loi 67–1253), 1967.
7
Urbanisme 138 (December 1974): iv.

Because most local authorities can't afford planning staff, master plans are usually prepared by planners from the ministry of equipment. These planners are in agencies called Atelier Départemental d'Urbanisme (ADU), which are part of the DDE. In the Paris region, the planners who staff the ADU's are on loan from the IAURP, the regional planning agency. They provide the necessary expertise to the local authorities and help keep the local plans consistent with the regional plans. Larger communes may prepare their own master plans, while others may hire private consultants.

As one would expect in France, the process of approval is rather complex. The master plans must be approved by the commune's municipal council, the prefect, the region, and the concerned ministries. However, each approval is a very elaborate exercise. At each step consultations are held with numerous agencies in an attempt to reach a consensus on the plan. Objections are accommodated if possible. The consultations are done in an atmosphere of semi-secrecy.[8] Only when a consensus has been reached among the various agencies is the plan published, although many public and private groups with a stake in the results attempt to find out what is in the unpublished plan. Once the plan is published public hearings are held. Although further modifications may be made, the announcement of a public hearing in reality means that the plan will not be drastically changed.

There are currently seventy-three SDAU's being prepared or approved in the Paris region alone, covering about one-half of the region's area and two-thirds of the population. Nine are for the five new towns (three each for Saint-Quentin-en-Yvelines and Marne-la-Vallée, and one each for Cergy-Pontoise, Evry, and Melun-Sénart).

The master plans do not tell the public precisely what changes can be expected; they are designed to give the general guidelines of development and the new infrastructure that will be located somewhere in the area. The quantity of such new investments is known but not the exact location. The function of precisely stating what uses and densities are permitted at particular locations as well as the exact location of public works projects is performed by the Plan d'Occupation des Sols (POS), comparable to American zoning ordinances. The POS, which must conform to the SDAU, explains in minute detail the current and future distribution of land uses and densities in the

---

[8] When the Paris master plan was being prepared in the mid-1960s the location of the proposed axes of development and the new towns was kept secret for as long as possible in order to discourage land speculation. Several maps were prepared with conflicting information so that if any became public the secrecy would still be intact.

area.[9] Like the SDAU, it may be developed by a single commune or by several together. About 360 out of the 1,305 communes in the Paris region are currently developing a POS, with over 100 more where work has not yet started. Many of these are in new towns. The POS is used primarily for communes that are already highly urbanized. Less built-up communes in the region are covered by a Plan Directeur d'Urbanisme Intercommunaux (PDUI), a detailed plan for several commune areas, which covers 90 percent of the region, although only 15 percent of the population.

Communes with relatively rapid increases in population can not conveniently use either method. The POS and PDUI are designed to present a "snapshot" of a relatively stable existing situation and the precise changes expected. In rapidly growing areas such as new towns the exact future arrangement of land uses cannot be known. Long-term master plans are feasible but local officials do not know precisely the intentions of private developers. Once the commune is no longer rapidly growing a POS can be imposed.

At first glance, this system appears to provide a relatively simple method for filtering national policy down to the regional and local levels. Placing regional and national "experts" in the local offices would appear to assure that national and regional directives are incorporated into the local plans. However, the POS and SDAU are very controversial documents in areas with strong development pressures. Private developers oppose plans that try to modify the direction of existing growth; they prefer to build in the area of "natural" growth, that is, through continuous extension.

In the Paris region the pressures are particularly acute because the regional master plan is trying to reorient urban growth from a sprawling fashion (*tache d'huile*) to the two axes. The promotion of axes requires the control of development in the land between. Suburban communes located outside the axes of development proposed in the regional master plan have become battlegrounds for private developers and landowners trying to promote new projects not in the plans and national and regional planners trying to preserve the axes concept by concentrating development in new towns. The strongest battle to preserve the axes is being waged in the western region, where the most expensive suburban projects are located. Landowners could realize much higher prices and developers could construct expensive homes if planning permission were given.

9. "The Urban Development scheme or SDAU defines the main lines of action and the Ground Occupation Plan or POS gives them legal form; the SDAU guides, while the POS specifies; the SDAU announces, but the POS schedules." *Urbanisme* 138 (December 1974): iv.

Local officials are vulnerable to the pleas of private developers to make a small exception in the POS just for them. Many local officials have close relationships with private developers and find that the best way to secure a high-paying job in the private sector is to demonstrate how they were able to get planning permission for a project. The national and regional planners, more removed from these pressures, look at the total impact of all master plans. The SDAU's and POS's are designed to be in conformance with the regional plans, such as the one already described for the Paris region, but the net effect of many small exceptions made for individual developers is to violate the intentions of the regional plan.

Land acquisition and price freezing: The ZAD system

The cornerstone of the economic rationale for new towns is that because development is to take place on rural land the original cost of that land will be substantially cheaper than if development were to take place within the continuously built-up area. A lower land price enables the consumer to enjoy lower rents and taxes. Over the long term, prices in the new towns will rise to the same level as elsewhere in the region, but the big increases will go to the development corporation, not private landowners. The biggest problem in practice is that an announcement of intention to construct a new town sets off increases in land prices before the developer owns the land. At Columbia, Maryland, the developer, James Rouse, secretly acquired the 15,000 acres through several dummy companies before he revealed plans for the new town. As a result, land was acquired at near agricultural value. Publicly sponsored new towns, however, cannot use secrecy in land negotiations.

To keep down the cost of land needed for new urban projects, in 1962 the French adopted a technique called Zone d'Aménagement Différé (ZAD), a deferred development zone. ZAD is an attempt to find a middle position between the right of the state to expropriate at its current value land needed for public improvement and the right of private landowners to be compensated for the future profits denied them by the government action.

The ZAD technique freezes land at its value one year before the designation. Any local authority, EPA, or national agency may declare a ZAD. If an owner wishes to sell his "ZADed" land to another private individual, the public authority that has declared the ZAD has the right of first refusal to buy the land at the asking price. If that price is roughly the same as the frozen value then the public authority is not likely to intervene. If it is considerably higher — usually at least 25 percent above the frozen price — there is likely to be public intervention. The public authority has the choice of matching the asking price, negotiating for another agreeable price, or initiating expropriation proceedings. The ZAD declaration lasts for fourteen years. Once a piece of land has been under the ZAD system for three years the owner can demand that the public authority acquire the land through negotiations or expropriation. If that authority refuses, the land must be revalued at a new (presumably higher) level and then refrozen for fourteen more years.

The ZAD system is used for two purposes: first, to ensure low prices for land to be acquired for urban improvements, either in the short run or far in the future; second, to "throw a monkey wrench into" land transactions in locations where urban development is undesirable. The government cannot stop urban development using only ZAD, but the technique at least delays and complicates land speculation.

About 136,500 hectares of land were under ZAD control in the Paris region in 1974, 11.4 percent of the region's total land area. Figure 4–1 shows the location of ZAD areas in the Paris region and the five new towns. The largest ZAD designation — about 40 percent of the total — is in the southwest corridor, to prevent speculation along future expressway routes. About one-fourth of the total "ZADed" land is in the five Paris new towns. The remaining amount is in a variety of areas, including residential, recreational, and commercial.

The amount of land actually acquired is far less than the area under ZAD. In the five Paris new towns, 10,810 hectares had been acquired by 1974, compared to 36,463 hectares under ZAD control. Table 4–1 compares the pace of land acquisition in these new towns with the amount under ZAD and the total areas of study and intended urbanization. About one-half of the land in the new town ZAD's has been acquired, with most of the rest under ZAD controls at the moment. In fact, more ZAD areas have been designated than will ever be used for new town development. The other ZAD designations are designed to dampen speculation near the new towns.

Because of the local government fiscal crisis, land acquisition must be financed nationally. Funds are derived from loans taken out by the local authorities from FNAFU (an interministerial committee whose resources come from the CDC) or from direct grants from the Ministry of Equipment. Approximately 1.1 billion francs was expended on land acquisition in the nine new towns by the end of 1974, of which some 632 million came from state grants and 468 million from loans. The land acquisition costs have amounted to about 800

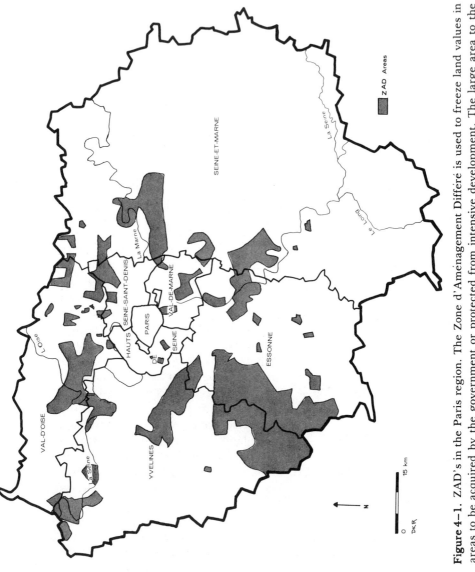

Figure 4–1. ZAD's in the Paris region. The Zone d'Aménagement Différé is used to freeze land values in areas to be acquired by the government or protected from intensive development. The large area to the southwest of the Paris region was designated to protect the right of way of an autoroute.

Table 4–1. Land Situation in the Five Paris Region New Towns

Town	Original Study	ZAN	ZAD	Acquired	ZAC
Cergy-Pontoise	10,000	6,000	6,500	2,627	2,211
Evry	9,000	2,000	3,500	1,726	982
Marne-la-Vallée	17,000	5,000	6,500	3,824	2,803
Melun-Sénart	17,000	9,000	8,900	3,245	1,640
Saint-Quentin-en-Yvelines	16,000	6,500	11,000	2,863	2,760
Total	69,000	28,500	36,400	14,285	10,396

NOTE: The ZAN is the territory within which new development is to be concentrated. It corresponds to the area of concern of the SCA. The parts of the communes in the original study area already urbanized were not included in the ZAN unless they chose to join. The area under ZAD control is larger than the ZAN area of concentrated development in order to dampen land speculation on the fringe of the new projects. About half of the land in the ZAN areas has been acquired by the EPA's. Not much more land needs to be acquired. ZAC's have been created on around 10,000 hectares in the five new towns, about half of the total eventually planned. Land not included in the ZAC's will be used for open space.

million francs for the five Paris new towns and 300 million for the four provincial ones.

The ZAD system has worked fairly well in the new towns. Land has been acquired at an average price of $7,000 per acre in the Paris new towns and $5,000 per acre in the provinces. The prices paid by the new towns in the Paris area are five to ten times less than for land in outer suburbs not covered by ZAD and only one percent of the land costs in central Paris. However, ZAD effectively keeps down land prices only if the public authority is committed to buying the land when market pressures are placed on the owner to sell well above the frozen price. When acquisition is not intended, the public authority can hope that the ZAD designation will dampen private speculation because of the potential threat of government expropriation if the prices go too high. The antispeculation strategy is used on the periphery of new towns, but inside the new towns the land is being acquired. The land in the new towns is resold to private developers with the exception of the town center, which is leased to private developers rather than being sold. As the commercial and employ-ment core of the new towns, the town centers will yield most of the anticipated profits associated with urban development. As the value of the town center land increases in the future, higher rents will be charged.

Two particular problems have developed in the use of the ZAD's. First, landowners have found that by submitting to expropriation proceedings they are likely to receive much higher compensation than the frozen value. Most judges in France apparently are sympathetic to the notion that the seller is entitled to a portion of the surplus value, even though the buyer is a public agency. Because expropriation takes a very long time, the land has a chance to increase in value a bit more before settlement. Thus, the price actually paid by the public agency will be a compromise between acquisition at agricultural and fully speculative levels.

The second problem is that the ZAD procedure is toothless unless the government preemption threat can be backed up with acquisition when necessary. If the public agency does not have the money to buy the land if demanded by the owner after three years, then the owner is free to sell at a speculative price.

Joint public-private development agreements: the ZAC system

The third fundamental land development tool is the Zone d'Aménagement Concerté (ZAC), a mechanism for public-private cooperation in the provision of needed services and facilities. This system has proved useful in dealing with two fundamental obstacles in the French urban development system. The first problem is the lack of coordination between local authorities and private developers. In a liberal economy, where the private sector is responsible for the provision of new housing, coordinating mechanisms are needed to ensure that public services will be available for new residents or firms.

Under the traditional relationship between the public and private sectors, if a developer wants to construct a large project he first applies for a permit. If the commune gives the developer the permit, the project would be finished before the local authority could organize the construction of needed roads, sewers, schools, swimming pools, etc. The only way to assure comprehensive development in a liberal economy is to negotiate in advance of development.

The second problem is the system of financing the supporting services. As I have stated, local authorities do not have an adequate tax base to pay for new services from local revenues. The commune must therefore borrow money, even if the required amount exceeds its ability to repay. The new projects could generate tax revenue to repay the loans, but the local authorities must spend the money for the new services prior to the arrival of the new taxpayers. In many cases, new residents will demand more in social services than they pay out in taxes, especially if the new residents have a low income.

A mechanism for formal coordination is extremely useful for the national planners. The priorities in awarding grants and loans to local authorities serve as a tool for implementing a national urban growth policy. Uniform procedures of applying for the infrastructure grants would assist in the process of creating priorities. The challenge was to create a mechanism that would enable local authorities simultaneously to plan new projects in cooperation with private developers and to receive assurances from the government concerning the subsidies needed for infrastructure.

The system created in the 1950s in France to deal with the coordination and financing issues was the Zone d'Urbanisme en Priorité (ZUP), a priority development zone. With the ZUP procedure, the local authorities received financing from the appropriate ministries to develop the services required in designated zones of concentrated new urbanization. The procedure failed for two reasons. First, the ZUP did not provide for mechanisms of coordination with private developers. Second, the ZUP could only be initiated if the commune met financial guarantees. Virtually all communes were unable to meet the financial requirements before a ZUP could be approved. Even if approved, the ZUP required a large financial commitment by the localities, with state approval; loans from the state had to be paid off over a six-year period at 2.75 percent interest. This was insufficient time to permit the localities fully to recover the outlays through taxation.

The procedure that replaced ZUP is the ZAC, created in 1967. This procedure is a way for local authorities and private developers to face the problems of financing comprehensive development together anywhere in France, not just in the new towns. The developer is told by the local authority that if he wants his project he will have to make some sort of contribution toward the provision of public facilities. This contribution could be direct payments, donation of land for public buildings, construction of the buildings for the local authority, etc. In return for assuming a share of the infrastructure costs, the private developer usually receives a tax concession. This arrangement increases the likelihood that utilities will be ready in time, but it gives developers a long-term bonus in the form of lower taxes.

The division of benefits between the private developers and public authorities depends on the relative negotiating competence of the two and the level of market pressure on the site. If the proposed project for a particular location is attractive for private investors then the local authority can negotiate a favorable contract. On the other hand, where demand is relatively low, local authorities must give greater financial inducements. In the new towns the EPA's do most of the negotiations. Although they have a high degree of technical competence, they are limited in the bargaining process by the fact that most of the new towns are located in areas with relatively low market pressures. The EPA therefore must frequently make concessions to attract developers.

Once the private developer and local authority or EPA have negotiated a ZAC agreement, it must be approved by either the prefect of the department, the regional prefect, the minister of equipment, or the prime minister, depending on the size and importance of the particular project. Approved ZAC's receive top priority for infrastructure grants from the government. Because it is now extremely difficult to initiate a large project in France outside a ZAC area, the selection of approved sites constitutes a significant element in a national policy for the location of urban growth.

Virtually all construction in the new towns is located in a ZAC. However, the mere designation of a ZAC area does not mean construction is assured. The private builder, having agreed to a financial arrangement with the commune or new town concerning the provision of public services, is not actually bound to provide the housing and services at a particular speed; the pace of development is still governed by the market. ZAC's located where demand is greatest for new housing or industry will be developed most quickly. Partially in response to the uncertain pace of development, the EPA's are directly managing some ZAC's themselves. This strategy has usually been applied to the town centers, the focal points that the EPA's wish to develop rapidly regardless of short-term consumer demand. The EPA's contract directly with builders and lease the land instead of selling it.

The ZAC system is a bitterly controversial one. Defenders of the program argue that, given the problem of insufficient local government financial capacity to fund the necessary public works in France and the relatively inefficiency of trying to finance them through taxation in advance of development, the ZAC system represents a practical way to tap the private sector for the needed financing. The shriller opponents call the ZAC a sell-out to private developers. The criticism is based on the nature of the contract between the local authority and the private developer. The ZAC system was supposed to avoid the rigidity of the POS system. In ZAC areas the POS does not apply, although the SDAU, which sets the overall planning goals for the district, is still in effect. In reality the ZAC system too has proven inflexible. The contract typically calls for the contribution of a fixed sum by the private builder for the construction of infrastructure. What happens if the actual cost of infrastructure is more than anticipated? The private developer has signed a contract calling for a fixed contribution. The cost overruns must then come from the financially strapped local authority. The local authority is back in the same financial bind as before, but without the benefit of zoning control over the site or the possibility of collecting taxes from the builder.

Although virtually all construction in the new towns is done through the ZAC method, three other kind of private–public cooperation have been used:

1. the sale of land with a covenant to respect. This is the most frequently used method in France. The private developer must conform to certain uses, methods of construction, and density. A similar procedure is sometimes used in the United States. The sale of land with a covenant works only if the market is strong enough to encourage private developers to initiate building activities. Such has generally not been the case inside the new towns.

2. associations from the time of the studies. In certain cases where a large-scale project is envisioned, the EPA's have brought in private developers at the planning stage in order to reconcile possible conflicts between the new towns planning objectives and the economic needs of the developers. This sort of relationship has occurred in a few situations. At Marne-la-Vallée, several developers together worked on the master plans for the sector of Noisiel, one of three SDAU's created for Marne-la-Vallée. The developers prepared financial feasibility estimates and assisted with the preparation of detailed plans for the residential district.

At Saint-Quentin-en-Yvelines the future urban center, including residential and commercial space, was studied by a group of private financial experts. At Le Vaudreuil the first section of the new town, with 5,000 dwelling units and an employment zone, was the subject of experimental planning and construction techniques. Private enterprise cooperated in the planning studies and in industrial construction for housing.

3. competitions. Innovative ideas and younger, less established architects can be attracted through design competitions. Competitions are much more common in Europe than in the United States for large public projects. Architects submit plans based on guidelines established by the public agency (the EPA in the new towns). Competitions are particularly useful when many functions are to be combined in one large structure, because the result could be an unusual megastructure. Competitions have been held at Evry and L'Isle d'Abeau for large housing projects.

QUANTITATIVE IMPACT OF THE NEW TOWNS PROGRAM

The planning tools described here have proved to be a mixed blessing for the new towns. The lack of land suitable for immediate development, due to the chaotic system of financing infrastructure, has provided the planners with a lever for influencing the location of urban growth. This lever has been strong enough to divert some growth to the new towns but not to prevent development where market pressures are greater. The planning tools have facilitated the construction of both new towns and competing projects. Despite the planners' efforts, the new towns have not achieved the desired quantitative impact. The number of new homes and jobs attracted to the new towns has fallen considerably behind the announced goals.

In 1969 the four-year-old SDAURP was revised. The main difference was a reduction in the number of new towns in the Paris region from eight to five (table 4–2). Two of the eight new towns — Mantes and Beauchamp — were eliminated altogether, primarily because of intense opposition from the affected communes. These two were expected to contain about 750,000 people by 2000. The new towns of Southeast Trappes and Northwest Trappes were combined into a single new town, named Saint-Quentin-en-Yvelines. The total number of people expected to be housed in this area was reduced from about 900,000 to 300,000. The projected populations of Cergy-Pontise and Marne-la-Vallée were reduced from 700,000–1,000,000 to about 300,000. Melun-Sénart was cut from 500,000 to 300,000. Only Evry, at 500,000, remained unchanged. Overall, the Paris new towns program was reduced from 4.5 million inhabitants anticipated in 2000 to 1.73 million.[10]

The Paris region should grow from about 8.5 million in 1962, 9.3 million in 1968, and 10.0 million in 1975 to 14 million in 2000. The designated areas of the five new towns are planned to grow from about 400,000 residents in 1968, to 1.73 million in 2000, an increase of 1.3 million. This represents about 28 percent of the total anticipated growth of the region. By contrast, in the original 1965 master plan, the eight new towns were expected to grow from 110,000 in 1962 to 4.5 million in 2000, comprising 80 percent of the total regional growth. One-eighth of the 14 million residents of the Paris region in 2000 will live in the five new towns.

The British experience since World War II can demonstrate the degree of realism in the French goals. During the 1950s the London new towns designated in the late 1940s grew by 235,860, while the southeast region of England grew by 1,144,000. The new towns therefore comprised about 20 percent of the total growth in that decade. Southeast England grew by 959,000 in the 1960s, while London new towns added 167,506, or 17.5 percent of the total growth.

[10] These changes were officially incorporated into the master plan of 1975 (Préfecture de la Région Parisienne, *Schéma directeur d'aménagement et d'urbanisme de la région parisienne, Avril 1975* [Paris: Préfecture de la Région Parisienne, 1975]).

Table 4–2. Reduction in the Size of the Paris Region New Towns

1965 Master Plan		1969 Revised Master Plan	
New Town	Population (in thousands)	New Town	Population (in thousands)
Beauchamp	300– 500		
Cergy-Pontoise	700– 1,000	Cergy-Pontoise	330
Evry	300– 500	Evry	500
Mantes	300– 400		
Noisy-le-Grand	700–1,000	Marne-la-Vallée	300
Tigery-Lieusaint	400– 600	Melun-Sénart	300
Trappes northeast	300– 400		
		Saint-Quentin-en-Yvelines	300
Trappes southeast	400– 600		
Total	4,500	Total	1,730

NOTE: Between the publication of the 1965 master plan and the initiation of construction around 1970, the size and number of new towns in the Paris region were reduced.

In Britain as a whole, the new towns captured 14 percent of the national growth between 1950 and 1970, 341,290 out of 2.4 million in the 1950s and 356,608 out of 2.5 million in the 1960s.

The Paris new towns are currently planned to take 28 percent of the growth of the Paris region, a higher percentage than that achieved in southeast England or Britain as a whole. The French effort is optimistic based on the British experience yet not infeasible if the planning controls work. The 1965 master plan, which allocated 80 percent of the Paris region's growth in new towns, was clearly unrealistic based on London's experience.

The sixth plan called for 114,790 housing starts in the five Paris new towns between 1971 and 1975, an average of just under 23,000 per year. The goal for the five new towns represented about 22 percent of the total anticipated housing starts for the Paris region. The new towns were thus expected to attract about 28 percent of the population increase and 22 percent of the housing starts in the Paris region. The discrepancy is due to the fact that new houses are being built in central Paris to replace demolished substandard units.

Table 4–3 shows the extent to which the five Paris new towns met the objectives of the sixth plan program for housing starts.[11] The

[11] The French do not generally monitor housing starts per se. Instead, they are concerned with *dotations* and *financements engagés*. *Dotations* are the annual appropriations for housing assistance offered to the builders by the government. *Financements engagés* are the funds actually accepted by the builders in a given year. The year that ground is broken for a new housing project may not coincide with the year in which the financing is secured. However, from the point of view of the new

Table 4–3. Housing Starts in the French New Towns, 1971–75

New Town	Goal*	Reality	Percentage of Goal Achieved
Paris region			
Cergy-Pontoise	23,800	10,100	43.9
Evry	17,740	10,505	59.2
Marne-la-Vallée	23,300	8,584	36.8
Melun-Sénart	23,000	4,727	20.6
Saint-Quentin-en-Yvelines	26,950	16,900	62.7
Total for Paris region	*114,790*	*50,816*	*44.3*
Provinces			
Etang-de-Berre	27,500	20,100	73.1
Lille-Est	6,150	6,539	106.3
L'Isle d'Abeau	6,750	2,967	44.0
Le Vaudreuil	6,500	2,810	43.2
Total for provinces	*46,900*	*32,416*	*69.1*
Total	*161,690*	*83,232*	*51.5*

*The goals came from the sixth national plan.

goal of the sixth plan was for 114,790 housing starts in the five Paris region new towns between 1971 and 75. During that five-year period, however, only about 50,000 housing units were under construction, about 44 percent of the sixth plan goals. The least number of housing starts occurred in 1971 (8,000) and the most in 1972 (16,000). The situation varies from one new town to another. At Saint-Quenten-en-Yvelines and Evry about 60 percent of the goal was achieved, compared to 20 percent at Melun-Sénart.

The differences among the new towns can be measured by three factors: the date of initiation of the project, the distance from central Paris, and the attractiveness of the new town within the particular submarket of the Paris region. Despite the fact that it is further from central Paris than three other new towns and has been delayed by local opposition, Saint-Quentin-en-Yvelines has 50 percent more housing starts than any other Paris new town. Its strength is due entirely to its location on the western side, the most dynamic submarket in the Paris region. The western suburbs are considered the most attractive environmentally, a consequence of the historical extension of attractive residential areas in central Paris toward the Bois de Boulogne. Saint-Quentin-en-Yvelines, however, is marketed

towns planners, once the financial situation is settled there is little more they can do to get the project built.

not as a new town, but as "near Versailles." About one-fourth of the housing starts in the department of Yvelines have been concentrated in Saint-Quentin-en-Yvelines.

The second strongest new town is Evry, the one considered by most observers to be the most "successful" of the five. Evry is in the midst of the fastest growing corridor in the Paris region, to the south of central Paris. It has the best communications links with Paris, via the national autoroute to Lyon and the Riviera and the first new rail line built in France in fifty years. The prefecture of the new department of Essonne was located in the town. Evry is located near a number of large housing projects that have grown without adequate nonresidential services nearby. It is thus becoming a service center for a subregion. Planning started early at Evry and development has proceeded at a steady, deliberate pace. Its market is not as attractive as Saint-Quentin-en-Yveline's, but the location, communications, head start, and prefecture are Evry's advantages.

Cergy-Pontoise was the first new town to be started and, like Evry, it has a prefecture. These are its only two advantages, however. Communications are poor and its submarket is known to be relatively unattractive because of the particularly large percentage of low-income, highrise projects. Marne-la-Vallée has the advantage of being located closest to the center; however, the east side of Paris is attractive only to low-income families who have been priced out of the west. Housing conditions among residents currently living in the east are poorer than elsewhere in the region. Marne-la-Vallée has suffered considerable construction delays by its lack of fast transportation links to Paris until late 1977. Melun-Sénart has few advantages: it is the last new town to be started, the furthest from Paris, and the worst served by transportation links. Its one major attraction is the fact that because of its relatively isolated location and low land prices it can offer primarily single-family dwellings, an increasingly popular style of living for the French.

In contrast, the four provincial new towns have achieved 80 percent of their goal. The sixth plan programmed 46,900 housing starts between 1971 and 1975. In reality, about 32,416 have been started. The strong showing among the provincial new towns is due primarily to the pace of development of Berre, which accounts for nearly two-thirds of the activity in the provincial new towns. Pressures for new housing have been strong in Berre because of the fast growth of the new port facilities at the nearby Gulf of Fos. Over 4,000 units per year have been started there. The university town of Lille-Est is exceeding its original sixth plan goal of 6,150 housing starts during the five-year period. Le Vaudreuil is having the most trouble getting started.

Unlike the other three provincial new towns, it is not located adjacent to a large new employment center.

Although the Paris new towns are not reaching their goal of approximately 23,000 housing starts per year during the sixth plan, the Paris region as a whole is achieving its goal of just over 100,000 per year. It is clear that other parts of the region must be attracting more than the anticipated growth to counteract the observed shortfall in the five new towns.

In fact, the number of housing starts in all locations within the Paris region has exceeded the sixth plan goal (table 4–4). In central Paris, the sixth plan called for the construction of around 12,000 dwellings per year; the actual number of starts has been around 14,500. In the inner suburbs, the goal was around 39,500 and the reality 40,500. For the outer suburbs other than the new towns, the goal was around 30,000 and the actual starts around 38,000. The new towns were supposed to attract 23,000 per year but have averaged only 10,000.

The conclusion is clear: the shortfall in the achievement of the sixth plan housing goals is primarily due to a failure to capture housing starts, which went elsewhere in the outer suburbs of the Paris region. About 43 percent of the 53,000 housing starts for the outer suburbs were supposed to be in the new towns; in reality, only 24 percent have been there. The new housing has instead been located in scattered and semirural sites, in ZAC's, and in projects located on the periphery of the new towns.

It is fairly difficult for the planners to curtail construction of the 15,000 low-density, single-family houses in the outer suburbs. Builders of these units require only a building permit from the local authorities. Because no subsidies or grants are involved the national government has no method of control over the amount of such housing. Furthermore, about one-half of the 15,000 scattered houses are built as second homes for weekends or vacations, because the outer departments of the Paris region extend into rural areas.

The true competitiors of the new towns, and the beneficiaries of the shortfall in reaching the goals of housing starts in new towns, are the ZAC projects and other high-density suburban projects. Although the overwhelming majority of the housing in new towns is contained in ZAC's, the system is being used successfully elsewhere in the region as well, where private market development pressures are stronger.

There are sixty-three ZAC's inside the area of concern of the five EPA's of the Paris new towns and another eighteen within the original study areas but outside the current EPA and SCA boundaries. These eighty-one have been designed for an eventual capacity of about 220,000 dwellings according to the agreements signed by the

Table 4–4. Distribution of Housing Starts in the Paris Region

Location	Goal 1971–75	Achieved 1971–75	Acieved 1975	Estimate 1976–77
Central Paris	12,000	14,500	26,000	39,000
Inner suburbs	39,500	40,500	34,000	62,000
Outer suburbs (not including new towns)	30,000	38,000	31,000	56,000
New towns	23,000	10,000	11,000	18,000
Total	104,500	103,000	102,000	175,000

NOTE: The table shows the goals established in the sixth national plan for annual starts within the Paris region and the actual achievement. All parts of the region exceeded the sixth plan goals, with the exception of the new towns. Since 1975, however, housing starts have declined in the inner and outer suburbs and increased dramatically in central Paris.

EPA's and private developers and approved by the national government.

In the outer suburbs of the Paris region other than the new towns, 142 ZAC's have been created, with planned capacity of 250,000 dwellings. Of these ZAC's, forty-seven have been located withing two miles of the new towns, with a capacity of about 110,000 dwellings. Although a few of these projects were in fact approved before the initiation of the new towns in the late 1960s, most have been started since then. The ZAC's in the new towns have developed more slowly because developers prefer the ones elsewhere in the outer suburbs (see table 4–5).

Pressure to reduce the scope of the new towns program has originated with governmental sources as well as private developers. The most critical period in the survival of the new towns policy came in the late 1960s. Political opposition within the government came from three sources: regional planners who sought to reduce the importance of Paris, local government officials who feared the loss of autonomy, and the "economic liberals" led by Chalandon who considered new towns to be inefficient. These three groups did not kill the new towns concept, but the net effect of the various attacks has been a sharp reduction in the size of the new towns.

The national planners in the DATAR were suspicious of the new towns idea because it was perceived as a Paris-oriented policy. The new towns were first advocated for the Paris region in the 1965 master plan, and their chief supporters were the regional administrators. The DATAR was committed to a policy of opposing large-scale growth of the Paris region. Instead, they said investments for new housing and jobs should be made elsewhere in the country in order to

Table 4–5. ZAC's in the Paris Region New Towns and Elsewhere in the Outer Suburbs

New Town	Within Development Area[1]		Within Study Area but Outside Development Area[2]		Within 2 mi. of Study Area	
	ZAC's	Dwelling Units	ZAC's	Dwelling Units	ZAC's	Dwelling Units
Paris region						
Cergy-Pontoise	8	34,975	1	1,250	16	25,899
Evry	9	20,397	8	17,394	4	2,707
Marne-la-Vallée	9	37,450	4	5,818	10	25,503
Melun-Sénart	22	52,907	0	0	6	14,814
Saint-Quentin-en-Yvelines	15	45,839	5	5,140	11	39,026
Total	63	191,568	18	29,602	47	107,949
Other outer suburbs					95	142,846
Total ZAC's in the outer suburbs					223	471,965

NOTE: Less than half of the ZAC's in the outer suburbs are found in the five new towns.

[1]"Within Development Area" refers to the approximate area of concern of the EPA's and SCA's.

[2]"Within Study Area, Outside Development Area" refers to the original study area used for planning purposes in the 1960s.

reduce interregional disparities. The diversion of large sums of money for the construction of new towns in the Paris region could run counter to that effort.[12] Despite their misgivings about compromising their policies on growth in Paris, however, the DATAR officials did eventually support the new towns in both Paris and other regions of the country. Many observers attribute this change in attitude to the

[12]According to Delouvrier,

I was very hesitant to take the name "new towns," because it was easy to foresee that the words "new towns" would have certain consequences. If it were said that new suburbs were being built in the Paris region no one would have said a thing; but the term "new towns" is a pretension, a method of organizing true growth. Everyone in the provinces and even in the government was going to take this as a desire to see the Paris region grow. For this reason I hesitated, but I thought that if I didn't take the name there would be so many obstacles, particularly financial, to be overcome in the creation of true new towns that if we didn't have a special name for the exceptional actions the minister of finance wouldn't agree to give us a sou. Without the special name he would be obliged to give all the money for new suburbs. Thus, after hesitating I said, "Let's take the name 'new towns' and then channel everyone's efforts — architects and administrators — into the promotion of an innovative idea." (Interview with Paul Delouvrier, July 1974, my translation.)

influence of Paul Delouvrier. As the head of the Paris region during the 1960s, he was the leading advocate of the new towns. He is said to have sold the DATAR on new towns as an appropriate tool for making the *métropoles d'équilibre* concept operational.

Regardless of the extent of Delouvrier's influence, the alliance between the DATAR and the Paris region in support of new towns was primarily due to the common threat posed by Chalandon. When Chalandon became minister of equipment in 1968 he expressed skepticism as to the usefulness of the new towns. He constantly threw at the new towns supporters remarks such as "Where are the new towns?" or "I don't see anything." Chalandon put the Paris regional planners on the defensive. He succeeded in removing Delouvrier from office in 1968 and installed a new set of leaders. Support for new towns in the Paris regional governmeent, however, unexpectedly increased. With Delouvrier gone, the Paris regional assembly was forced to evaluate the merits of its policies in the face of strong criticism from the national level. It became clear that the only policy uniquely their own was that on new towns. Everyone built roads and schools, while the new towns represented the only program that would not logically be run at the communal or departmental levels. When the Paris regional officials asked themselves, "What do we have of value?," the answer was "New towns." After eight years no other activity justified the continuation of a strong regional government in Paris.[13]

Despite the strong stand taken by the Paris regional officials in favor of new towns, the Chalandon attack on the new towns could have proven lethal. The new towns gained a reprieve because the issue became subordinated to a more significant planning controversy. If Chalandon's attacks on the planning system had drawn opposition only from the planners in the Paris region and the DATAR, the new towns policy could have been stifled. However, local government officials around the country felt threatened by Chalandon's criticism of the permit system. Local officials consider the right to grant a permit for the construction of all new buildings to be their most potent power. No project can be undertaken without the approval of the commune and department.

To Chalandon the reluctance of local authorities to issue permits was primarily responsible for the lack of sites for new projects. He called for the elimination of the permits to be replaced by market allocation of the needed land. This effort was strongly opposed by the powerful local government lobby in France, led by the minister of

[13]Interview with J.-E. Roullier, June 1974.

interior. Local authorities were wary of the new towns for a number of reasons. Those where new towns were to be located faced financial hardships and an eventual loss of identity. For others, the new towns constituted a potential threat to their ability to decide how much growth should take place within their boundaries. However, whereas the new towns represented a potential and isolated threat to local officials, Chalandon's reforms would adversely affect all local officials immediately. In this light, the new towns represented the lesser of two evils for the local government lobby.

The new towns thus were nurtured through the upheavals of the late 1960s by the Paris regional planners, despite the removal of the strongest advocate and the opposition of national and local officials. The new towns survived because the regional officials strongly defended them after Delouvrier left and because the national planning controversies revolved around other issues.

I have identified the reasons why housing starts in the French new towns, especially those in the Paris region, have fallen short of the stated goals. The primary problem is the nature of the French development process. Including the private sector in the construction of new towns inevitably means that the demands of the market must be taken into consideration. The shortage of developable land, especially in the Paris region, gives the planners some influence over private sector location decisions. A number of planning tools have been devised to promote the timely and orderly urbanization of new areas by private developers. However, these public interventions cannot eliminate market influences. Private developers will invest in new towns only to the extent that the properties can profitably be sold to consumers. The result of this tension between market forces and planning controls is that housing is built in the new towns — certainly far more than would be without the public effort — but a much smaller percentage than has been considered desirable in the master plans.

Given the market "realities" of the Paris region, only very strong controls could succeed in bringing about the goals of the plans. There is no one in the Paris region, however, pushing for an increase in the pace of housing construction in new towns. I have stated that the developers prefer to stay away from the new towns if given the choice. Land with equipment is tight in the region, but for developers the advantages of avoiding the new towns still outweigh the disadvantages. By locating on the periphery of the new towns, housing developers can offer residents whatever services the new towns will have available while at the same time avoiding the taxes and controls of the new towns. Developers regard new towns as emergency reserves, available for construction if other sites cannot be found or if public policy makes it impossible to continue to find small sites for construction in the future.

Communal and departmental authorities in the Paris region are no longer as hostile to new towns as they were originally, but they tend to ignore the new towns unless directly affected. The treasured power to issue permits to construct houses remained with the communes; new towns pose a latent threat to that power, but not as great as the alternative of removing strong controls over the location of new development.

The national government has recognized the reality of the development trends in the Paris region in the seventh national plan. Goals for housing starts in the Paris new towns have been brought down to more realistic levels. The seventh plan calls for the construction of only 15,000 dwellings per year in the five Paris new towns, slightly above the reality during the years of the sixth plan but considerably below the sixth plans goals.

The most surprising aspect of this situation, however, is that the new towns planners themselves are not concerned by the slowness of development. Aware of the critical importance of securing the cooperation of private builders in the French development process, the planners are content to sacrifice the rapid pace of development for more critical goals, primarily social ones. The reasons why it is necessary to make a choice will become clear in the next chapter. Because the new towns planners are not unhappy with the slower pace, they have cooperated with the private builders' desires to use the new towns as an emergency resource. The three new towns in the Paris area where market pressures are potentially greatest—Evry, Marne-la-Vallée, and Saint-Quentin-en-Yvelines—have all reached agreements with a syndicate of developers, or, in the case of Saint-Quentin-en-Yvelines, with banks. The EPA's in these three new towns have given developers options to develop large tracts of land to be subdivided among the various members of the syndicate as any desire to use the land. In this way the developers bottle up the supply of developable land in the new towns with EPA blessings. ZAC agreements are concluded, with the EPA providing needed infrastructure and developers honoring the EPA's social goals. The two new towns most behind the goals—Cergy-Pontoise and Melun-Sénart—are the two where developers have been so reluctant to build that they are not even willing to enter into a syndicate to control the pace of development. The three new towns with syndicates are able to secure enough construction from the developers to satisfy the planners and to enable them to achieve social policies. The nature of these social policies will be examined in the next chapter.

The failure of the new towns to gain a larger percentage of growth is not due to a lack of funds. National grants have been available for infrastructure expenditures, including land acquisition and site prep- aration. The sixth plan budgeted about 1.1 billion francs for infra- structure between 1971 and 1975. The amount actually authorized has been about 900 million francs (correcting for inflation), over 80 percent of the goal. The new towns have received about 92 percent of the goal for water and sewer construction, 78 percent for primary roads, 71 percent for secondary roads, 81 percent for land acquisition, and 50 percent for open space. The Paris new towns have received 78 percent of their goals, compared to 86 percent in the provincial new towns (see table 4–6).

In contrast, state grants for superstructures have lagged well behind the targets of the sixth plan. The nine new towns have received 488 million francs for superstructures, 54 percent of the sixth plan goal of 908 million francs. The new towns have received about 65 percent of the budgeted aid for primary schools; 61 percent for sports facilities, around 52 percent for various health and social service facilities, and 45 percent for secondary schools. The Paris new towns have considerably lower percentages than the provincial new

Table 4–6. National Grants Committed to the New Towns Compared to the Sixth Plan Goal of 1971–75 (in thousands of francs)

Use	Paris Region		Provinces	
	Sixth Plan Goal	Reality	Sixth Plan Goal	Reality
Infrastructure				
Land acquisition	277,000	206,122	173,000	159,160
Primary roads	289,989	228,913	110,300	83,432
Open space	17,500	12,080	17,500	5,340
Secondary roads	0	0	21,600	15,436
Water and sewer	137,020	116,598	62,990	67,685
Total	721,509	563,713	385,390	331,053
Superstructure				
Primary schools	189,700	106,217	63,359	57,147
Secondary schools	271,330	91,356	105,503	77,479
Health facilities	68,332	23,518	27,606	25,474
Social equipment	29,926	12,481	9,580	8,088
Sports facilities	90,000	50,439	52,200	36,017
Total	649,288	284,011	258,248	204,205
Total	1,370,797	847,724	643,638	535,258

NOTE: Figures have been adjusted to allow for inflation.

towns. Overall, the Paris new towns have received 44 percent of the sixth plan goals, compared to 79 percent in the provinces. The disparity is strong for both levels of schools and health facilities, where little more than one-half of the goals have been received.

The reason for the lag with regard to superstructure but not infrastructure is that the superstructure equipment is dependent on the presence of a large population, whereas the infrastructure investment is a prerequisite before the population can be attracted. The shortfall in superstructure grants is due to the problems discussed above with regard to attracting a high percentage of the housing market. Water services, sewers, and roads are necessary before houses can be built, but the mere presence of utilities, even in a allegedly tight regional market for equipped land, is not sufficient to ensure growth.

5

ACHIEVEMENT OF
SOCIAL GOALS

The major social objective of new towns planning is the creation of a socially balanced community. New towns are offered as a tool to counteract the predominant patterns of social segregation found in urban areas. In this chapter, I will examine the success of the French new towns at achieving social balance, as measured in two ways. The first is through the presence of different social classes in proportions comparable to those found in society. The new town is designed to be a microcosm of society, not a one-class project. The second way is by the creation of a self-contained community, with all daily functions provided in appropriate quantities. The new town should contain enough jobs for the residents and, conversely, affordable homes for the workers, as well as adequate recreational and commercial facilities.

The notion that new towns should be built to promote social goals can be traced back to nineteenth-century utopians and businessmen. Many businessmen observed that industrial output was adversely affected by high absentee rates and low productivity among employees who were present. Workers were absent or ineffective because of poor health. Businessmen concluded that the physical conditions causing the unhealthy work force were not found inside the factories, for they thought it natural to expect people to work long and hard for wages. The problem began when people left the factory for the night and headed straight for the neighborhood pub. After having spent their money on the unhealthy activity of drinking, the workers would return to homes with no sanitary conveniences, little space or light, and little to eat except bread and potatoes. The unsanitary conditions and unhealthy habits of the work force outside working hours produced employees incapable of giving a full day's output.

In order to improve the moral lives of their workers and therefore improve productivity, some industrialists decided to build new factories away from the existing cities. The workers lived in new homes built by the businessman adjacent to his factory. These towns were designed to provide all of the services and facilities that the factory owner felt were beneficial to the workers. Schools, churches, shops, and recreational facilities were built but no pubs, gambling halls, or other ''unhealthy'' diversions. The towns had ample open space and modern sanitary facilities. These model industrial towns were built in many countries, including Saltaire, Bournville, and Port Sunlight in England; Guise and Noisiel in France; and Pullman in the United States.[1]

The other foundation for the new towns idea in the nineteenth century came from the utopians. The utopian tradition goes back to Plato's *Republic* and Thomas More's *Utopia*, which gave its name to the entire movement. In the nineteenth century a large number of utopians wrote in response to the problems of the industrial city. Critical of the way modern industrial society had developed, they proposed the construction of new communities in which the technological advances of the nineteenth century could be applied toward the creation and maintenance of an ideal society. One of the most influential French utopians was Charles Fourier, who called for the development of new communities based on a very complex social system. Fourier's ideal society was one in which class rivalries were subordinated to a universal harmony. Universal harmony required the elimination of limits on the expression of human passions. A community in which passions were allowed free play would easily attract followers because it was what people by nature prefer. People would live in a community called a phalanx. Each phalanx would contain 1,500–1,600 inhabitants and would be economically self-sufficient. The only building in the phalanx was the phalanstery, a large structure in which all of the citizens' needs and passions would be accommodated in a communal atmosphere.[2] Many utopians and their followers came to the United States to establish communities

---

[1] See Colin Bell and Rose Bell, *City Fathers: Town Planning in Britain from Roman Times to 1900* (New York and Washington, D.C.: Fredereck A. Praeger, 1969); Leonardo Benevolo, *The Origins of Modern Town Planning* (London: Routledge and Kegan Paul, 1967); Stanley Buder, *Pullman* (New York: Oxford University Press, 1967); Gordon E. Cherry, *Urban Change and Planning* (Henley-on-Thames: Foulie and Company, 1972); and Annick Brauman, *La Familistère de Guise* (Paris: Centre National d'Art et de Culture Georges Pompidou, 1976).

[2] Jonathan Beecher, *The Utopian Vision of Charles Fourier* (Boston: Beacon Press, 1971).

consistent with their social principles. The most famous was Brook Farm, Massachusetts.

Unlike Utopias and model industrial towns, new towns are designed not to change social relations radically but to capture within a small community the diversity of activities found in society at large. If French new towns were developed solely according to market pressures, only low- or lower–middle-income housing projects would be built there. This situation conforms to the pattern found in most areas of the world outside North America. High-income families in Paris, like other European cities, prefer to live in the center of the city, where services and facilities are the best and residents have easy accessibility to jobs and cultural activities. To compensate for the lack of private open space, upper-income urban dwellers maintain weekend homes in the nearby countryside. As a matter of fact, some of the worst highway congestion in Paris occurs on summer Sunday evenings when families return from their rural second homes. Lower-income families live in the suburbs because they have been priced out of central locations.

THE SOCIAL BALANCE PROBLEM

The meet the problem of a housing shortage after World War II, large-scale housing estates were built on the periphery of European cities. These projects, called *grands ensembles* in France, combined the disadvantages of both town and country—high-rise apartment living without the convenient accessibility to jobs and services. These one-class suburbs aggravated the social segregation problem, especially in Paris, by accommodating the increasing tendency for higher-income families to locate in the center and lower-income families on the periphery.

In contrast to the *grands ensembles*, the new towns have been consciously planned to promote social balance. The *grands ensembles* are built for one social class, while the new towns seek a wide variety of people; they have few recreation facilities and parks, while the new towns have a generous supply; they have inadequate commercial facilities, while new towns have large shopping centers; they have no jobs available on the site, while new towns are designed to be employment centers.

The problems of social segregation are in certain ways different in the United States. Two obvious differences can be perceived: the rich have tended to move to the suburbs, leaving the poor in the center, a reversal of the European pattern; and segregation by race as well as by income further aggravates the problems of spatial isolation in American cities. Although the precise spatial patterns may differ between American and European cities, the fundamental problem of widespread segregation of different social groups remains the same. Because the fundamental problem of spatial segregation is comparable, the use of new towns to achieve socially balanced communities is as relevant to the American situation as to the French.

The use of new towns to promote social balance has in fact been proposed by a number of American analysts in recent years. Anthony Downs, for example, has suggested that new towns be used to organize the dispersal of inner-city ghettos. Because of the hostility of many white middle-class families to blacks moving into their established suburban neighborhoods the most feasible way to secure suburban homes for low-income blacks, according to Downs, is in entirely new communities where there are no middle-class white families already on the site.[3]

The need to create socially balanced communities was recognized in the Title VII legislation. According to the act, new community projects receiving federal assistance had to make substantial provision of housing for low- and moderate-income families. As required by the act, HUD established the guidelines and standards to be met by private developers with Title VII assistance. The new town plan had to provide assurances that a mixture of housing types would be built during each major phase of residential development. The new town had to contain single-family houses as well as apartments, homes for sale and for rent, and housing suitable for families of all ages and sizes. New towns developers had to sign a contract with HUD agreeing to meet certain goals with regard to the percentage of lower-income housing before the loans and guarantees were released.

In the absence of governmental pressure and support, private developers cannot build socially balanced communities. The experience of James Rouse at Columbia, Maryland, illustrates the limit of private initiative in the field of social planning. Rouse proposed a number of social goals for Columbia, but the goals could not be achieved. The cost of new housing is too high for most American families without subsidies.

---

[3] Anthony Downs, *Opening Up the Suburbs: An Urban Strategy for America* (New Haven: Yale University Press, 1973). See also Richard Burton and Harvey A. Garn, "The President's 'Report on National Growth, 1972': A Critique and an Alternative Formulation," in U.S., Congress, House, Subcommittee on Housing of the House Committee on Banking, *Selected Papers* (Washington, D.C.: Government Printing Office, 1972).

When construction started at Columbia in the mid-1960s the developer proposed to provide a large percentage of units for low- and moderate-income families. In the early years of the city, a number of housing units were built for low- and moderate-income families. Because the cost of new housing is too high for most American families, lower-income families could be accommodated only through subsidies from the government. In the early years of Columbia subsidies were available through Section 236 of the National Housing Act. A number of nonprofit and church-related organizations were induced by Rouse to apply for Sec. 236 funds. Moderate-income townhouses and high-rises were built in Columbia during its first half-dozen years. Since 1973 no further lower-income projects have been built. This is due to the fact that the federal government froze the Sec. 236 program that year. Although the program has since been revived, other communities have higher-priority claims on the limited funds. Columbia is unable to provide further lower-cost housing because no government agency has been willing to subsidize the difference between the cost of new housing construction and the ability to pay of lower-income families. Lower-income families have also been priced out of nonsubsidized housing in Columbia by the rapid inflation in house prices there. Houses built in the late 1960s for $20,000 were selling for $50,000 by the late 1970s. The lowest-priced new housing in Columbia has risen from around $18,000 in the late 1960s to $40,000 in the late 1970s.[4]

Similarly, Columbia is not a self-contained community. Although it has been quite successful in attracting jobs, the employees generally cannot afford the housing there. As a result, there is substantial cross-commuting. The largely professional-class residents of Columbia commute to the Baltimore and Washington suburbs, while the labor force at Columbia lives elsewhere in the region.

The inability of Columbia to achieve its social goals does not indicate a failure on the part of the developer but rather the inherent difficulties of a project realized without government support. Columbia really represents the strongest effort made by a private developer of a new town to implement social goals. Private developers cannot be expected to provide housing below cost for low-income families without government support for the difference between the socially desirable cost and the actual cost to the developer. Nor can a private developer create an equilibrium between jobs and residences in the absence of government programs to influence the location of employment.

[4]For a description of Columbia's development, see Gurney Breckenfeld, *Columbia and the New Cities* (New York: Van Rees Press, 1971).

The experience of the Title VII new towns has not been significantly different from Columbia. Despite the requirements imposed by the law and HUD guidelines to achieve social balance, the Title VII developers have faced the same problems as described for Columbia. New towns developers who agreed to provide a substantial percentage of lower-cost housing have found it difficult to secure federal housing subsidies to construct the housing. Jobs have been difficult to attract without the help of government inducements.

In contrast to the American new towns experience, the French and the British have been able to achieve socially balanced new towns. Several studies have been undertaken of the British experience. B. J. Heraud showed that the social composition of the London new towns corresponded fairly closely to regional patterns.[5] Ray Thomas found that the degree of self-containment was generally higher in new towns than in unplanned towns of similar size and distance from the central city.[6]

This chapter will demonstrate that despite some problems the French new towns have achieved a considerable degree of social balance in only a few years. This relative success is important for American planners in view of the facts already established about the French new towns program. Even though private developers are responsible for the installation of housing and jobs in the new towns, social balance has been achieved. The results have been obtained because the new towns planners have placed a sufficiently high priority on the achievement of social balance, even to the point of sacrificing other goals, most notably with regard to a rapid pace of development. The French success can be traced to the more rational distribution of public and private-sector roles in the new town development process.

If new towns were judged solely on the basis of their quantitative impact on urban growth they would not be considered successful. The French new towns account for only about 15,000 out of 500,000 housing starts in the country. Even in the regions where the new towns are located the impact is less than 15 percent. The impact of the Paris region's new towns has been comparable to the London new towns experience since World War II. However, the new towns planners have sacrificed speed of construction for the sake of social balance. Because of their peripheral location the new towns run the risk of being all low- or all moderate-income housing projects. Social

[5]B. J. Heraud, "Social Class and the New Towns," *Urban Studies* 5 (1968).

[6]Ray Thomas, *Aycliffe to Cumbernauld. A Study of Seven New Towns in their Regions* (London: Political and Economic Planning, 1969); and Ray Thomas and Peter Cresswell, *The New Towns Idea* (Milton Keynes: The Open University Press, 1973).

balance can be achieved only if different income housing is simultaneously attracted to the new towns, as well as nonresidential functions that would otherwise tend to cluster in the center. To meet their quantitative goals the new towns would end up being low-income dormitory suburbs like the *grands ensembles*. In order to attract middle- and upper-income families and jobs, the new towns have discouraged low-income projects. The pace of construction of low-income projects has been kept at a level low enough to ensure that social balance is fostered in the new towns.

An example may serve to illustrate the principle involved. Let us suppose that at Cergy-Pontoise the goal is to develop 50 percent upper-income housing and 50 percent lower-income. Let us also assume that the goal is to construct 5,000 dwellings per year, 2,500 lower- and 2,500 upper-income. If developers are available to build 1,000 upper-income housing units and 4,000 lower-income units per year then the planners have their choice of policies. They can go along with the developers, thereby achieving the goal of 5,000 starts even though 80 percent would be lower-income, or they can issue permits for only 1,000 lower income units, thereby reaching only 40 percent of the quantitative goal but achieving the planned division between social classes. Next, let us assume that the goal calls for 5,000 dwellings and 5,000 new jobs per year in the new town. If entrepreneurs are willing to establish only 3,000 new jobs per year in the new town, the planners again face a choice of two alternative policies. They can meet the goals for housing while sacrificing the balance between the number of jobs and residents, or they can lower the number of housing starts to maintain the desired relationship between the number of new jobs and residents. Although the exact numbers are different, these choices correspond to the actual situation faced by the new towns planners. Given the two policy alternatives, the new towns planners have sacrificed quantitative impact for the sake of balance. This chapter is concerned with an evaluation of the effort by these planners to build socially balanced communities.

THE BALANCE BETWEEN
SOCIAL CLASSES IN THE NEW TOWNS

The first way in which social balance is achieved in the new towns is through the representation of different classes. A completely balanced community would be one where the distribution of social classes corresponds exactly to that of society as a whole. In theory, planned new communities are better able to achieve a desired mixture of social classes than traditional unplanned projects. I shall therefore compare the French new towns with the mixtures of social classes elsewhere.

The early results of the attempt to develop socially balanced new towns in France are encouraging. A special census conducted in Cergy-Pontoise and Saint-Quentin-en-Yvelines, the new towns with the largest number of new residents, determined the distribution of occupations of the household heads, using the standard French census categories. The surveys determined that the distribution of professions does not vary significantly from that found in the region as a whole: about 1 percent business executives, 8 percent professionals, 24 percent administrators, 23 percent clerical workers, 35 percent blue-collar workers, 4 percent domestic workers, and 4 percent miscellaneous (clergy, artists, and military) (see table 5–1). The Paris region has a higher percentage of business executives and fewer administrative workers than the new towns.[7]

Families in the new towns are larger than in the region as a whole. The average household size is 2.61 in the Paris region, compared with 3.15 in the new towns. Over half of the households in the region contain one or two persons, compared to one-third in the new towns. Conversely, one-third of the region's households but one-half of the new towns households contain three or four persons. However, the

Table 5–1. Profession of Head of Household in Cergy-Pontoise, Saint-Quentin-en-Yvelines, and the Paris Region

Profession	Cergy-Pontoise	Saint-Quentin	Paris Region
Agriculteur (farmer)	0.3%	0.3%	1.1%
Patron de l'industrie et du commerce (owner or executive)	0.7	0.7	7.7
Profession libérale et cadre supérieur (professional)	6.4	9.4	8.4
Cadre moyen (administrator)	22.2	26.5	14.9
Employé (clerk, secretary)	22.1	24.3	21.6
Ouvrier (blue-collar worker)	38.6	31.7	35.5
Personnel de service (domestic)	4.4	3.7	8.3
Autre catégorie (clergy, artist, military)	5.5	3.4	2.5

NOTE: Using the standard French census categories, it can be seen that the new towns are quite similar to the overall distribution in the region.

[7] Groupe Central des Villes Nouvelles, *Bilan*, p. 78; and *Informations d'Ile de France* 26 (1977): 32.

figures for the new towns are comparable to the average household size in the outer suburbs, 3.06. Central Paris, with an average household size of only 2.02, brings down the regional figures (see table 5–2).[8]

The new towns do show an imbalance in age distribution. They contain twice the regional average of individuals under 10 and between 20 and 29. Over 60 percent of the residents are in these two age groups, compared to 30 percent in the region. On the other hand, the new towns have fewer older residents: only 10 percent of the new towns residents are over 40 and 2 percent over 60, compared to 42 percent and 17 percent, respectively, in the region. Despite the small number of elderly individuals at this time, the new towns planners are still trying to provide services for them. Housing projects for the elderly have been integrated into neighborhood centers. In the long run, the age differences should lessen as the current residents grow older (fig. 5–1).[9]

Table 5–2. Household Size

Number in Family	New Towns	Paris Region
1	13%	25%
2	18	28
3	27	19
4	24	14
5 +	18	14

SOURCE: France, Groupe Central des Villes Nouvelles, *Bilan des villes nouvelles au 31 Décembre 1975, p. 77.*

The French new towns have attracted a socially heterogeneous population by offering a wide variety of housing. In France a reliable indicator of the likely social class of an occupant of new housing is the method by which the project was financed. There are three types of housing in France:

1. *Très aidé* (heavily assisted)—low-income housing built through a national program known as Habitation Loyer Modérée (HLM), moderate rental housing. Loans at 1 percent interest are made by the Caisse des Dépôts et Consignations. They are received either by housing authorities established by local governments or by nonprofit sponsors, such as church groups or labor unions. Some private profit-making developers also secure these loans; they agree to devote a portion of a large project to nonprofit housing in exchange

[8] Ibid.
[9] Groupe Central des Villes Nouvelles, *Bilan*, p. 76.

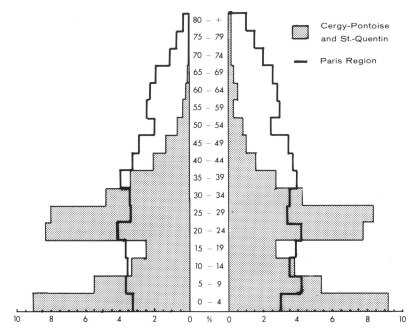

Figure 5–1. Division of population by age and sex in Cergy-Pontoise, Saint-Quentin-en Yvelines, and the Paris region. The pyramid shows an excess of residents in the new towns below age 10 and between 20 and 29, and a smaller percentage of residents above age 40.

for government approval and financing of the entire project, on which the developer will of course expect to make an overall profit. Rents are set to cover the cost of construction and maintenance with a profit. Because virtually all HLM projects consist of high-rise apartment buildings, in which construction costs do not significantly vary, rents will differ from one unit to another based on the cost of the land. An HLM building in central Paris will obviously have a much higher rent than in a peripheral location because of the enormous difference in land costs. Government rental assistance programs are available to some low-income families in HLM housing to reduce rents further. The national government, by deciding how many HLM projects will be built and where they will be located, exercises a dominant role in the development of low-income housing in France. A few experimental projects have departed from the normal pattern of high-rise rented apartments with low-rise or owner-occupied homes. These experiments constitute less than 5 percent of the total, however.

2. *Aidé* (other aided) — middle-income housing financed through a variety of government loans and loan guarantes. Private developers apply for direct government loans or guarantees for loans secured by

the developer from private financial sources. In either case the developer enjoys lower-cost loans than would be secured through the private market without government assistance. In exchange for the lower rates the developers agree to limit profits to 6 or 7 percent. The combination of lower-cost loans and limited profits keeps the house costs below the level of the private market. The loan guarantees are most frequently handled by the Crédit Foncier (mortgage land bank). *Aidé* housing is also financed through contributions by private industries. Companies with more than ten employees contribute 1 percent of their payroll to a housing fund. All styles of housing are financed under this program, including single-family and owner-occupied homes as well as apartments and rental units. As a result, housing costs to consumers can vary widely within this category.

3. *Non-aidé* (unassisted) — upper-income housing built without governmental assistance. This sector comprises single-family homes built in the suburbs, weekend homes in peripheral and rural areas, and downtown luxury apartments, especially in central Paris.

As was pointed out in Chapter 2, the Etablissement Public is prohibited from actually building housing itself; the task must be performed by either local authorities or private builders. As the landowner in the new town, the EPA negotiates with builders to construct the type of housing the planners wish to see on a particular tract. Thus, the EPA planners do not control the distribution of housing types through direct contruction but by releasing land to builders with agreements attached concerning the type of construction planned.

In recent years a little over 100,000 dwellings have been started annually in the Paris region, about 30 percent *très aidé*, 40 percent *aidé*, and 30 percent *non-aidé*. The percentage of *non-aidé* housing has been increasing in recent years at the expense of the other two categories. Since 1975, *non-aidé* housing has accounted for nearly half of the region's housing starts.

The three types of construction have not been evenly distributed throughout the Paris region. Central Paris, with about 25 percent of the region's housing starts, has less than 10 percent of the new *très aidé* and *aidé* housing and nearly half of the *non-aidé* housing. The inner suburbs have about 40 percent of the low-income housing starts and 30 percent of the middle- and upper-income starts. The outer ring contains half of the low-income, 60 percent of the middle-income, and less than one-fourth of the upper-income housing starts.[10] In other

[10]Préfecture de la Région Parisienne, *Région Parisienne*; and *Informations d'Ile de France* 26 (1977): 28.

words, in central Paris over 80 percent of the housing starts are *non-aidé*, compared to one-third in the suburbs. The distribution in the Paris region by method of financing thus accurately reflects the social-class imbalances noted earlier.

The distribution of housing starts in the Paris region can be compared to the effort in the new towns. Approximately 10,000 housing units have been begun each year in the five Paris new towns, about 10 percent of the region's total starts. About 30 percent of these were *très aidé*, 60 percent *aidé*, and 10 percent *non-aidé*. [11]

The distribution of housing starts projected for the Paris new towns is at variance with the rest of the region. The most significant difference is the relatively small percentage of *non-aidé* housing planned for the new towns. Around 40 percent of the Paris region's housing is built without government assistance, compared to 10 percent in new towns. Housing, as was pointed out before, is generally constructed by private builders, since the EPA is prohibited from building. Location of new *très aidé* and *aidé* housing projects can be influenced by the government through the process of financial assistance. This type of lever cannot be exercised in the housing sector where no public financial assistance is involved. Therefore, *non-aidé* housing is located according to market demands, while private decisions concerning the location of government-assisted housing can be manipulated if the public policy does not coincide with the market trends. *Non-aidé* housing is built where demand for high-income housing is the greatest. This area comprises central Paris, the near western suburbs, and the rural fringe. The market for high-income housing in the new towns is not as big.

The difficulties of the new towns in attracting unassisted housing can be further demonstrated by comparing the distribution of housing starts in the new towns with the pattern throughout the outer suburban area of the Paris region. The four departments that comprise the outer ring contain about 40 percent of the total housing starts in the Paris region and about one-fourth of the new *non-aidé* units. The five new towns represent about one-fourth of the outer ring's housing starts in the low- and middle-income categories, but less than 10 percent of the upper income starts. Thus, even if the outer suburbs were isolated from the region as a whole, the performance of the new towns in attracting the unassisted upper-income housing is poor. The new towns planners therefore must use the variety of housing starts with government financial assistance to achieve social balance.

[11] Ibid.

The relative lack of a market for the development of *non-aidé* housing in the new towns, even compared to the rest of the outer suburban ring, can be attributed to two sources. First, a significant percentage of the *non-aidé* housing in the outer suburbs is for isolated weekend homes on the rural fringe. A second reason is that although *non-aidé* housing is not being demanded as part of the new towns plans, the new towns are in fact attracting the upper-income housing near them. Upper-income housing is available near the new towns in two ways. First, developers are constructing new *non-aidé* projects adjacent to the new towns. These projects are either American-style detached dwellings or else garden-style apartment complexes with a high level of amenities. These projects offer easy access to the large shopping centers being planned outside of Paris, including the new towns. The residents of these projects apparently desire automobile access to good retail facilities but prefer not to live in the heterogeneous environment of a large town or in high-rise apartment buildings.

A second phenomenon is the tendency for higher-income residents wishing to live close to the new towns to reside in one of the old villages within the designated areas. Because the designated areas are large, the new town construction activities are concentrated in several focal points, leaving many small villages unaffected. Structures in these villages have been renovated by upper-income residents. This type of activity is particularly strong at Cergy-Pontoise, where old homes in the picturesque town of Pontoise have been favored by businessmen and by the planners themselves, who have offices in the new town.

On the other hand, new towns planners permit fewer *très aidé* projects than are demanded. *Très aidé* developers are very eager to build in the new towns because of the method of financing HLM housing. HLM projects are nonprofit ventures with the rents set at the level to repay construction costs at a 1-percent interest rate. Virtually all HLM *très aidé* housing consists of high-rise apartments. For large builders, the construction costs generally do not vary from one site to another. The only exception is land costs; the higher the land acquisition costs, the higher the rents that must be charged. Because land in the new towns is at least one hundred times cheaper than in the central cities and inner suburbs, rents are much lower for HLM projects in the new towns than elsewhere.

Although integration of social classes is most easily correlated with the mix of financial assistance, a variety of residents is sought by building different styles of structures. In the Paris region less than one-fourth of the houses are single-family units, most of which are old structures or weekend homes. The historic preference for very high density apartment living remains strong in the Paris region, but demand has increased for American-style single-family homes, a trend now supported by government policy. As recently as the late 1960s, only 10–15 percent of the housing construction in the Paris region was single-family, but by the mid-1970s the figure had reached 20–25 percent. The new towns in the Paris region have sought to attract this growing market for single-family houses. Nearly one-third of the housing starts in the five new towns have been single-family units, with the figure projected to reach 40 percent in the late 1970s. The percentage varies from 25 percent at Saint-Quentin-en-Yvelines to 46 percent at Melun-Sénart. As was the case with HLM housing, the main attraction of the new towns for builders is the availability of a large supply of relatively low-cost land (see table 5–3). [12]

One indication of the attractiveness of new towns for single-family, owner-occupied housing is the frequent use of the special HLM program for home-owners. The program comprises less than 5 percent of all HLM housing starts in France and about 15 percent in the Paris region; HLM for owners comprises one-third of the total HLM starts in the new towns. (HLM for owners counts as housing that is *aidé* rather than *très aidé*.) Similarly, the percentage of owner-occupants is higher in the new towns than the Paris region as a whole. About one-third of the new towns residents are owner-occupants, compared to less than 20 percent in the region. [13]

Table 5–3. Distribution of housing starts in the Paris New Towns and Paris Region by Type of Assistance, 1971–75

	Très Aidé	*Aidé*	*Non-Aidé*	*Single Family*
Cergy-Pontoise	33%	59%	8%	29%
Evry	19	69	12	33
Marne-la-Vallée	34	52	14	32
Melun-Sénart	24	60	16	46
Saint-Quentin-en-Yvelines	28	60	12	25
Total new towns	*28*	*60*	*12*	*31*
Paris region	22	32	46	19
Central Paris	14	15	71	0
Inner suburbs	40	30	30	9
Outer suburbs	38	44	18	40

[12]Groupe Central des Villes Nouvelles, *Bilan*, p. 12.
[13]*Informations d'Ile de France* 26 (1977): 28.

The significance of the attempt by the new towns to achieve a mixture of housing types can be demonstrated by comparing the new towns with the *grands ensembles*. In virtually all of the *grands ensembles*, housing was constructed using only one kind of financial assistance; they are generally almost 100 percent *très aidé* or *aidé*. In a few of the larger projects a modest amount of variety was attempted but the homogeneous pattern predominates. Of the fifty-three largest *grands ensembles* only five had a complex mixture of different types of housing assistance. There were sixteen projects with nothing but HLM housing and eighteen with nearly all HLM. Two *grands ensembles* had entirely *aidé* housing and two more had almost completely *aidé* housing. Six were predominantly sponsored by nonprofit organizations and four by professional building societies. No housing in *grands ensembles* has been individual single-family housing, and only 5 percent of the occupants of *grands ensembles* are owners.[14]

The reason for this lack of variety is that the *grands ensembles* are built by only one developer—an HLM organization, SCIC, or other group—who has obtained financial assistance for the project as a whole. In the new towns, the developer is the EPA, which then contracts with numerous private builders for particular projects inside the new towns. Each individual project therefore has its own separate financing. The correlation between the homogeneous population and the lack of variety in housing style and financing in the *grands ensembles* alerted new towns planners to maximize the choice of housing.

CREATION OF A SELF-CONTAINED COMMUNITY

New towns planners can promote communities balanced between the middle and working classes by ensuring a mixture of housing types. The problem is how to attract the middle-class families, who demand a certain level of services and amenities in their environment. The new towns planners have sought to attract the middle class through the provision of a high quality of recreation facilities, good shops, and above all, adequate employment opportunities. These nonresidential activities not only promote a balance among social classes by helping to attract the middle class but they also contribute to the other determinant of social balance, the creation of a self-contained community.

[14]Paul Clerc, *Les Grands Ensembles*, p. 73.

Paris could never be replaced as the social and entertainment capital of the nation. The new town thesis, however, is that for most people, the facilities associated with being the national center — the museums, opera, etc. — are only used on infrequent occasions. The new towns need only be a convenient distance from the capital to allow access to these facilities when necessary. For routine daily activities — work, grocery shopping, athletics — one need not live in central Paris. Instead, a properly designed new town would allow an individual to fulfil virtually all his needs without having to travel long distances. Consequently, the new towns are designed to have large-scale downtown areas, where nonresidential activities are concentrated.

By far the most important method of promoting self-containment as well as attracting the middle class is through the types of employment opportunities offered. However, new towns planners have also sought to achieve these goals through the creation of high-quality shopping facilities and a wide range of recreational activities. Before discussing the employment situation in the new towns, I will describe briefly how the new towns have used these two functions.

Provision of Shopping Facilities

The new towns are achieving considerable success with regard to the provision of retail facilities. Historically, one of the problems faced by many new towns was the inadequate supply of stores in the early years. The lack of shopping facilities discouraged the addition of new residents, while the lack of residents discouraged retailers from opening stores. This problem has been dealt with through subsidies to retailers, the opening of temporary stores, or direct operation of stores by the new town development corporation itself. None of these methods has been entirely successful.

In contrast to this traditional situation, the shopping facilities in the French new towns are strong attractions for new residents. The reason for this fortunate position for the new towns derives from the extreme concentration of retail services in central Paris at the time the new towns program was formulated. In 1970 Paris contained 25 percent of the region's population, but 50 percent of the stores larger than 500 square meters, 82 percent of the stores larger than 2,500 square meters, and all of the big department stores. Although food could be bought near home, virtually all larger purchases were made in central Paris. As the Paris region continued to expand in area and population, the result of this pattern was to aggravate congestion in the shopping center and impose longer journeys on the suburbanites.

The construction of some suburban shopping centers in France dates from only around 1964. The pioneering company was Carrefour, which built a number of *hypermarchés* in France.[15] These stores, smaller than a department store, contain large supermarkets and an equivalent of a Woolworth's. Other firms began to construct a variety of new suburban shopping centers, including *superettes* (food stores of 120–400 square meters), *supermarchés* (food stores of 400–2,500 square meters), and *magasins populaires* (self-service, low-cost variety stores, like K-Mart, of 2,000–3,000 square meters). Between 1964 and 1972, 889,270 square meters of new stores were opened in the Paris region, of which nearly 85 percent were in the suburbs. Over 90 percent of the *hypermarchés*, *supermarchés*, and *superettes* were in the suburbs, and two-thirds of the *magasins populaires*.[16]

The proliferation of these so-called medium-sized shopping centers aroused considerable opposition among existing small shopkeepers, who rightly perceived these new shopping areas as a direct threat to patronage of existing suburban stores. Small shopkeepers in France have considerable influence in local politics. They have succeeded in cutting off the further spread of small shopping centers in the suburbs. The interest of the small shopkeepers has been reflected in the creation of administrative machinery to control new shopping centers. All proposed commercial centers with more than 1,500 square meters of sales floor space (or 3,000 square meters of all space) must be submitted to the Commission Départemental d'Urbanisme Commercial for approval. There is one commission for each department in France, consisting of twenty members: nine local officials (including the mayor in whose commune the project is proposed), nine local businessmen, and two representatives of consumer organizations. This system replaced one in which the prefect of the department was primarily responsible for issuing the permit. The 1,500-square-meter limit represents a direct attack on *hypermarchés* and other large stores. In view of the strong representation of local business interests it is easy to see how difficult it will become for new Carrefours to be built. In fact, the Carrefour company has turned to expansion in foreign countries.

Small suburban shopping centers were attacked because the shopkeepers saw them as stiff competition. At the same time, the planners recognized that the suburbs still needed new retail facilities to compete with the functions performed in central Paris. The

[15]An *hypermarché* is a store larger than 2,500 square meters, entirely self-service, with one-third of the space for food sales.

[16]*Bulletin d'information de la région parisienne* 11 (1974).

suburbs did not need *hypermarchés* of 2,500 square meters but large shopping centers containing department stores and services otherwise available only in central Paris. These new regional shopping centers would thus help reduce congestion in the center and improve the level of services in the suburbs.

The Paris district planners adopted a plan in the late 1960s for the creation of fifteen regional shopping centers, to be located near expressway interchanges and to have large parking lots to facilitate access by car. Each is planned to contain at least 50,000 square meters (in comparison, the mall at Columbia, Maryland, is 10,000 square meters). The structures themselves have covered malls to encourage entertainment and "sidewalk" cafes. On a typical Saturday the centers are extremely congested, both in the parking lots and inside the mall. In addition to normal consumers these centers are filled with promenaders, sightseers, and window-shoppers.

The first regional center, called Parly II, opened at Le Chesney, southwest of central Paris, in 1969. The volume of sales and visitors has far exceeded predictions. Since then ten other centers have opened, including those at the new towns of Cergy-Pontoise in 1973, Evry in 1975, and Noisy-le-Grand, part of the new town of Marne-la-Vallée in 1978 (see figure 5–2). A center will be completed at the new town of Saint-Quentin-en-Yvelines in the early 1980s. Commercial centers are also planned for the new town of Melun-Sénart, but construction is not expected to begin until the 1980s. The regional shopping centers serve as the commercial "downtowns" for the new towns. At both Cergy-Pontoise and Evry, the shopping center is located near offices and recreational facilities. The different elements are connected by pedestrian decks and walkways and are served by common parking lots.

As of January 1976, the five Paris new towns had over 160,000 square meters of commercial space in shopping areas of at least 5,000 square meters. Another 120,000 square meters was programmed for the 1976–80 period. Substantial progress has been made at Cergy-Pontoise and Evry, where regional shopping centers are open, and Saint-Quentin-en-Yvelines. The start of construction of the regional shopping center in Marne-la-Vallée was delayed several years after the department store chosen to anchor the project went bankrupt. The sixth plan had called for the construction of 307,000 square meters, so that the five new towns have in fact achieved over half the goal, including the projects under construction at the end of the sixth plan. Evry and Saint-Quentin-en-Yvelines have achieved their sixth plan goals with regard to the provision of commercial space. Cergy-Pontoise has reached 70 percent of its goal, while Melun-Sénart and Marne-la-Vallée have none (see table 5–4).

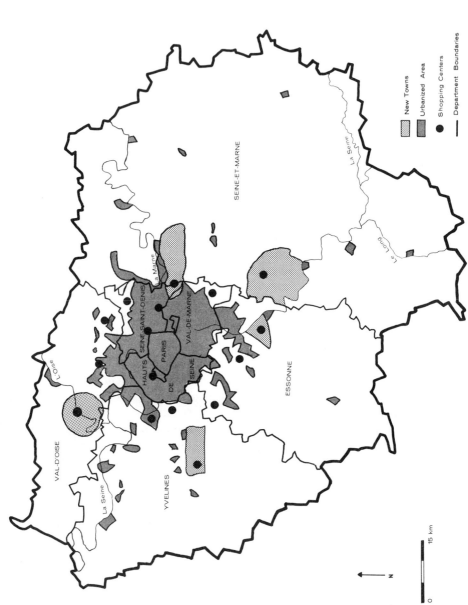

Figure 5-2. Shopping centers in the Paris region.

VAL-D'OISE

L'Oise

La Seine

YVELINES

SEINE-SAINT-DENIS

La Marne

HAUTS
DE
SEINE

PARIS

VAL-DE-MARNE

SEINE-ET-MARNE

La Seine

Le Loing

ESSONNE

New Towns

Urbanized Area

Shopping Centers

Department Boundaries

0   15 km

N

Table 5–4. Shopping Facilities with at least 5,000 m^2 under Construction in the New Towns, 1971–75

Town	Amount (m^2)	Percentage of Sixth Plan Goal	Seventh Plan Goal (m^2)
Paris region			
Cergy-Pontoise	53,000m^2	68%	36,000m^2
Evry	70,000	93	0
Marne-la-Vallée	0	0	55,000
Melun-Sénart	0	0	23,000
Saint-Quentin-en-Yvelines	38,700	129	6,000
Total Paris Region	161,700m^2	53%	120,000m^2
Provinces			
Etang-de-Berre	7,500	30	41,000
L'Isle d'Abeau	0	0	10,000
Lille-Est	0	0	0
Le Vaudreuil	0	0	16,500
Total provinces	7,500m^2	10%	67,500m^2
Total new towns	169,200m^2	44%	187,500m^2

NOTE: The regional shopping center at Marne-la-Vallée was under construction in 1977 and completed in 1978.

The situation is less positive in the provincial new towns. The sixth plan called for the initiation of 75,000 square meters during the five-year period. However, as of January 1975, only 7,500 had been built, all at Berre.

The new towns shopping facilities have been successful on both planning and financial grounds. From a planning view the shopping facilities are enabling the new towns to become self-contained and balanced communities. New towns residents will not need to travel into central Paris to shop in large department stores or smaller specialty shops. The new towns are able to offer a very large range of stores and to assemble a larger number of stores per person than almost any other area within the Paris region, with the exception of central Paris. In the Paris suburbs, there are about 0.37 square meters of commercial space for each inhabitant. Within the new towns, the figure is over 1 square meter per inhabitant.

The reason that the new towns can offer so many stores per capita is that suburbanites not living in the new towns use the shopping facilities as well. Even if planned new towns were not being built, regional shopping centers would have been located near the new towns anyway. The new towns shopping centers draw customers from a wide area. The first new town shopping center at Cergy-Pontoise, for example, contains the only department stores northwest of central Paris. When the center opened in 1973 there were 350,000 people living within twenty minutes by car, although only 10,000 were residents of Cergy-Pontoise. The center is located at an expressway exit and is much closer than central Paris for residents in the northwest quadrant of the region.

For the new towns, the shopping centers are proving financially attractive. Because of the large market area and the small number of centers permitted, private developers are anxious to build and operate the new towns shopping centers. In contrast to the housing and employment sectors, the new towns are able to deal with private developers from a position of strength. That is, the right to build and/or manage shopping centers in the new towns is an attractive proposition for private developers. As a result of this demand, new towns planners can secure an arrangement that is financially profitable for the new town as well as for the developers.

The Cergy-Pontoise shopping center was built by a private developer on land sold by the EPA. It makes an annual contribution to the new town based on a percentage of the income generated in order to pay for the management of the parking lots. With the demonstrated success of this shopping center, the other new towns have made more favorable financial arrangements. At Marne-la-Vallée, for example, the EPA negotiated directly with the large Paris department stores. After having obtained commitments from two department stores, it arranged a competition for the rights to attract the small stores, construct the facility, and manage it for seventy years, after which it would revert to the EPA or its successor. The first phase of construction included 40,000 square meters of shops and 15,000 square meters of office space. The project was delayed, however, when one of the department stores went bankrupt.

In contrast, the *grands ensembles* are lacking in adequate shopping facilities. Of fifty-four large *grands ensembles* in France with more than 1000 dwelling units, only twenty-five had a supermarket and six a cinema. Of four types of stores — commercial centers, supermarkets, neighborhood stores, and markets — 7 percent of the *grands ensembles* had none, 28 percent had only one of the four types, 44 percent had two, 19 percent had three, and 2 percent had all four. Several of the new large shopping centers have been located in *grands ensembles* in an effort to correct this deficiency. [17]

The new towns planners have benefited from the mistakes of the *grands ensembles*. The new towns are providing shopping centers at the same time as housing. Furthermore, the new towns shopping centers are financially successful because they can attract patrons from the underequipped *grands ensembles* of the outer suburbs.

[17]Clerc, *Grands Ensembles*, pp. 81–83.

Commercial facilities have been attracted to the new towns by a combination of powerful support from small shopkeepers and the pressures of market trends. Thus, the interests of the powerful small shopkeepers, whose views dominate national and regional policies for the location of commercial facilties, coincide with those of the new towns. By limiting the number of regional shopping centers and by severely constraining the ability of developers to build new *hyper-marchés*, the small business interests have given great benefits to those locations where new centers are allowed. Of the fifteen shopping centers planned for the Paris region, five are located in the new towns. If the current policies continue the new towns will achieve their objective of becoming commercial "downtowns" for the outer suburbs.

Recreational Facilities

The polls show that the reason most families like the new towns is the closeness of the countryside. Parks, sports facilities, and swimming area are especially important to families with children. Although central Paris has several famous parks, they are used primarily for passive activities such as walking, sitting, or playing bowls. There is a severe shortage of space for active recreation such as swimming or football. Furthermore, the French urban parks tend to be formal, with paths, gardens, and fountains, but little space for informal or spontaneous behavior. One arrondissement in central Paris actually has no park space. Although central Paris is the most attractive location for accessibility to jobs and cultural activities, the new towns can offer superior recreational facilities. Three types of recreational facilities are being offered in the new towns:

1. Smaller-scale equipment — This category includes sports fields, gyms, swimming pools, etc. The five Paris new towns receive about 5 million francs per year for small-scale sports equipment, about 20 percent of the total spent in the Paris region.[18] The new towns have had to compete with built-up parts of the region, where existing facilties are inadequate or deteriorated. Standards have been established for the appropriate per capita needs. The new towns have been able to meet these standards, in view of the relatively slow increase in population and high level of expenditure for recreational facilities.

2. Larger-scale regional recreational areas — Fourteen *bases de plein air et de loisirs* (regional leisure centers) have been designated in the Paris region, as shown in figure 5–3. These leisure centers are large complexes designed to offer a wide variety of recreational

[18]Préfecture de la Région Parisienne, *Région parisienne*, p. 76.

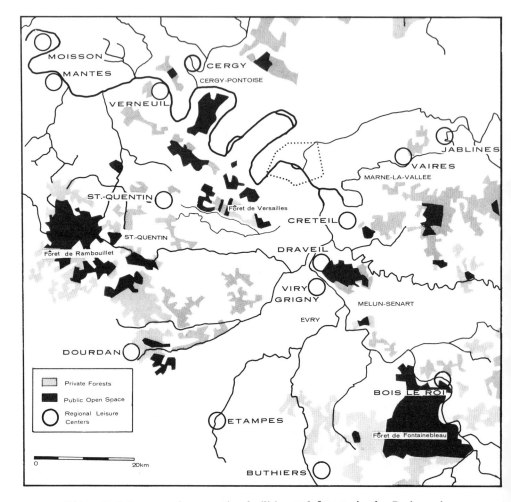

Figure 5–3. Large-scale recreation facilities and forests in the Paris region. Three-fourths of the forests are privately owned and not open to the public.

activities, including sports, swimming and boating, culture, and nature trails. The arrangements for financing the recreational areas are fairly complex, as an observer of French administration might expect. The communes and departments where the facility is planned form a syndicate at the insistence of the national government. This syndicate oversees planning and development of the site. The local authorities are expected to contribute 20 percent of the development costs. The rest is divided equally between the district and the national government.

The fourteen parks range in size from 65 hectares to 600 hectares. Together they constitute about 3,000 hectares. By 1977, 1,334 hectares had actually been acquired, with the rest awaiting the allocation of funds. Two are located within the new towns of Saint-Quentin-en-Yvelines and Cergy-Pontoise. The *base de loisir* at Cergy-Pontoise is located on a peninsula formed by the horseshoe-shaped meandering of the Oise River. The site is a low-lying area that will eventually be surrounded by the new housing and commercial projects on the other side of the Oise. The recreational area contains swimming pools, active sports fields, and hiking trails. The Saint-Quentin-en-Yvelines recreational area is dominated by a large lake for swimming and boating.

There are six other recreational areas within a mile or two of the new towns. Two of the projects are located along the Marne River, just north of Marne-la-Vallée. The Viry-Grigny recreational area is within the boundaries of the original study area for Evry but outside the current SCA territory. Melun-Sénart is bounded on the north and south by recreational areas. Another is located just west of Cergy-Pontoise along the Seine.

3. Forests and undeveloped natural areas — There are about 230,000 hectares of forests within the boundaries of the Paris region but only about 60,000 hectares are open to the public. The other forests are privately owned and not available for public use. The Paris regional government and the national government have sought to acquire forests both to make them available to the public and to prevent construction there by private owners. The state allocated 336 million francs in the sixth plan for the acquisition of around 10,000 hectares of forests.[19]

The new towns are all close to forests. The new town of Melun-Sénart in particular contains two very large forests whose preservation is desired by the government. The other new towns of the Paris region were located along the axes of urban development, which were carefully designed to minimize the intrusion of new projects into the forests.

Employment in the new towns

Superior social and commercial facilities play an important role in the promotion of self-contained new towns, but by far the most

[19]See Préfecture de la Région Parisienne, "Espaces boisés," map no. 4. Many private owners of forests are unable to maintain them. The government prohibits them

important element is the attraction of new jobs. A key goal of the French policy is to establish new towns that are job centers. The presence of a large number of jobs in the new towns could counteract the predominant trend in the Paris region toward the concentration of employment opportunities in the center.

The *grands ensembles* were criticized for their lack of job opportunities. Workers must leave the *grands ensembles* in the morning, travel a considerable distance, usually by train, and return to their apartments in the evening. The new towns thesis is that having jobs in the new towns would be beneficial to the workers because reduced commuting time produces less wear and tear on the individual and increases leisure time. Workers could be less separated from other members of the family. They could easily eat lunch at home in the French tradition or make full use of the town's leisure facilities.

Between 1971 and 1975 the five Paris new towns attracted about 45,200 new jobs, an average of 1,800 jobs per year for each new town and 15 percent of the total employment growth in the Paris region. Three of the Paris new towns are developing into strong employment centers — Saint-Quentin-en-Yvelines, with 13,400 new jobs through 1975; Evry, with 11,600; and Cergy-Pontoise, with 11,100. Melun-Sénart and Marne-la-Vallée have attracted only 6,300 and 2,800 jobs respectively. These two towns have developed more slowly because they are located on the east side of the Paris region, opposite from La Défense and the other strong employment locations.

The five new towns now contain about 0.9 jobs for every new house and about 0.64 new jobs for every new resident active in the labor force. The results have not been uniform among the five new towns (see table 5–5). Cergy-Pontoise and Evry have achieved ratios of approximately 1.1 new job for every new residence, or 0.8 jobs for every new resident active in the labor force. The ratio of jobs to dwellings is 1.32 at Melun-Sénart, the last of the five to begin construction. The ratios are much smaller at Saint-Quentin-en-Yvelines and Marne-la-Vallée. The former has the largest numbers of both new housing and jobs but for political reasons has had more difficulty than the other new towns in shutting off pressures for low-income housing construction. Marne-la-Vallée is located on the east side of the region, in the opposite direction of the strongest pressures for business location. Excluding Marne-la-Vallée, the other four Paris region new towns have attracted about 42,000 dwellings and 42,400 jobs through 1975, a ratio of precisely one new job created

---

from developing the forests, so that there is little they can do with them except watch them deteriorate.

Table 5–5. Ratio between Number of Jobs Attracted to the New Towns and Number of Housing Starts, 1971–75

New Town	Goal			Reality				
	Jobs	Dwelling Units	Jobs per Dwelling Unit	Jobs	Percentage of Goal	Dwelling Units	Percentage of Goal	Jobs per Dwelling Unit
Paris region								
Cergy-Pontoise	35,000	23,800	1.47	11,065	31.6	10,100	43.9	1.10
Evry	30,500	17,740	1.72	11,630	38.1	10,505	59.2	1.11
Marne-la-Vallée	22,400	23,300	0.96	2,845	12.7	8,584	36.8	0.33
Melun-Sénart	20,000	23,000	0.87	6,250	31.3	4,727	20.6	1.32
Saint-Quentin-en-Yvelines	24,000	26,950	0.89	13,430	56.0	16,900	62.7	0.79
Total	131,900	114,790	1.15	45,220	34.3	50,816	44.3	0.89
Provinces								
Etang-de-Berre	34,000	27,500	1.24	19,400	57.1	20,100	73.1	0.97
Lille-Est	7,160	6,150	1.16	2,560	35.8	6,539	106.3	0.39
L'Isle d'Abeau	6,400	6,750	0.95	2,690	42.0	2,967	44.0	0.91
Le Vaudreuil	4,000	6,500	0.62	1,200	30.0	2,810	43.2	0.47
Total	51,560	46,900	1.10	25,850	50.1	32,416	69.1	0.80
Total	183,460	161,590	1.13	71,070	38.7	83,232	51.5	0.85

for every house constructed, or 0.72 jobs for every new resident active in the labor force.[20]

In comparison there are now around 1.6 jobs per resident active in the labor force in central Paris and 0.6 in the outer suburbs. Thus, in a period of less than a decade the Paris new towns have become job centers, with a higher ratio of jobs to residents than in the outer suburbs as a whole. The London new towns begun after World War II achieved a surplus of jobs over residents active in the work force around 1960. The French new towns, begun twenty years after the British Mark I new towns, will have trouble achieving a surplus of jobs by 1980. On the other hand, the balance between new jobs and residents achieved in the new towns in just a few years is far greater than in the *grands ensembles*, most of which contain only a handful of jobs.

[20] Groupe Central de Villes Nouvelles, *Bilan*, pp. 8–16.

This balance between the number of jobs and the number of residents attracted to the new towns has been maintained in large measure by a policy of restricting the number of housing starts in the new towns. The sixth plan called for 161,690 housing starts in the nine new towns between 1971 and 1975 and 183,460 jobs, a ratio of 1.13 jobs per household. In reality the nine new towns attracted 83,232 housing starts and 71,070 jobs during the five-year period, a ratio of jobs to households of 0.85. Thus the ratio of jobs to households actually achieved is 75 percent of the sixth plan goal, while the percentage of housing starts achieved is 51 percent of the goal and the percentage of jobs created is 39 percent of the sixth plan goal. The balance between housing starts and new jobs was retained as a major objective of the seventh plan. For the period 1976–80 the plan called for the creation of 133,900 new jobs and 125,846 housing starts, a ratio of 1.05.

In seeking an overall balance between the number of jobs and residents, the new towns planners are also aware that the types of jobs attracted will have an impact on the distribution of social classes. The French planners therefore have two objectives. First, they wish to secure enough jobs to provide employment opportunities for all residents, the specific goal being to achieve a ratio of one between the number of jobs and the number of residents in the work force. Second, they seek a balanced distribution among different types of jobs. The danger to the achievement of social balance is that the new towns would become entirely low-income projects. As was pointed out, the market patterns in the Paris region favor the development of low-income rather than middle-income housing in the new towns. The difficulty in preventing a predominance of low-income residents is heightened by the fact that the easiest jobs to attract are industries and warehouses, which tend to have the lowest-paid employees. If the new town planners were concerned only with the overall ratio between jobs and residents the new towns would have few middle-class jobs and resident. The most effective mechanism devised to attract the middle class is to ensure that middle-class jobs are present in the new towns. These jobs are found primarily in the tertiary sector. Consequently, the employment attraction program in the new towns is largely an office-attraction program. By concentrating on attracting offices the planners can influence both the balance between jobs and residents and the balance between classes.

Over half of the Paris region's tertiary-sector employment is concentrated in central Paris. The government has encouraged offices to locate in the suburbs or provinces with indifferent results. On the other hand, new factories and warehouses are no longer built in central Paris. Most new factories built in the Paris region are for firms relocating from the center to the suburbs because of a lack of space for expansion in the center. The distribution of new jobs in the Paris region thus parallels the housing trends noted earlier. Higher-income office jobs further concentrate in the center while blue collar jobs are moved to the periphery.

Between 1971 and 1975, the five Paris new towns reached agreements for the construction of around 1 million square meters each of offices and factories and around 600,000 square meters of warehouses. Over 85 percent of the office permits were given for Cergy-Pontoise, Evry, and Saint-Quentin-en-Yvelinés. Melun-Sénart and Marne-la-Vallée have had more difficulty in attracting office developers because they are located in the eastern part of the region; offices attracted to the outer suburbs are much more likely to prefer a western location. In contrast, Marne-la-Vallée has attracted its share of new factories and warehouses, which are not as influenced by the psychological need to be in the west. Only Melun-Sénart, the most peripheral new town and the last to be started, has had difficulty attracting factories and warehouses. (See table 5–6.)

In the Paris region as a whole, about 42 percent of the jobs are in the secondary sector, comprising manufacturing and warehouses, while 58 percent are in the tertiary sector — offices and services. The number of tertiary-sector jobs has been increasing by about 50,000 per year in the Paris region while the number of secondary-sector jobs has been constant. Through 1975 the distribution of jobs in the new towns has been 45.8 percent tertiary and 54.2 percent secondary.

Table 5–6. Construction of Nonresidential Structures, 1971–75 (in square meters)

| Location | Agreements | | | Office Starts | |
	Industry	Warehouses	Offices	Achieved	Goal
New towns					
Cergy-Pontoise	343,970	94,141	314,933	191,900	128,000
Evry	194,594	143,520	265,762	128,900	162,000
Marne-la-Vallée	238,861	123,763	87,346	0	100,000
Melun-Sénart	44,799	35,010	56,719	22,220	45,000
Saint-Quentin-en-Yvelines	218,649	227,883	270,006	84,150	130,000
Total	1,040,873	613,317	993,766	427,170	565,000
Paris region	4,535,000	4,863,000	6,704,000		
Percentage in new towns	23.0	12.6	14.8		

Despite the fact that the number of tertiary-sector jobs is increasing while secondary-sector employment is stagnant in the Paris region, the new towns have more problems attracting tertiary-sector jobs (see table 5–7).

To counteract these trends various tools have been developed:

a. Limits on new office permits. New firms require a permit to locate anywhere in France. In the Paris region, the number of permits issued for new offices in a year has been limited first to around one million square meters and more recently to 700,000. Between 1971 and 1975, the five Paris new towns received about 15 percent of the total permits granted in the Paris region for offices and warehouses and 23 percent for factories, though by 1975 about one-third of all agreements were concentrated in the five new towns, compared to only 5 percent for central Paris. The decline in permits for central Paris is partly a reflection of the nation's economic conditions in the late 1970s, which resulted in a sharp drop in construction of office space by speculators. However, the decline is also due to the fact that more requests for permits are refused in central Paris than elsewhere. In 1975, nearly 30 percent of the requests for permits in central Paris were turned down, compared to 9 percent in the new towns, 2 percent in the department of Hauts de Seine (where La Défense is located), and 20 percent in the region as a whole.

Table 5–7. Distribution of Jobs between Secondary and Tertiary Sectors

	Jobs	
Town	Secondary Sector	Tertiary Sector
Paris region		
Cergy-Pontoise	61	39
Evry	41	59
Marne-la-Vallée	45	55
Melun-Sénart	40	60
Saint-Quentin-en-Yvelines	69	31
Total Paris region	*54*	*46*
Provinces		
Etang-de-Berre	69	31
L'Isle d'Abeau	61	39
Lille-Est	23	77
Le Vaudreuil	75	25
Total provinces	*63*	*37*
Total new towns	*58*	*42*

SOURCE: Groupe Central des Villes Nouvelles, *Bilan*, p. 16.

Although permits were issued for nearly one million square meters of offices, only 427,000 square meters were actually under construction in the five new towns. This shortfall is due to the fact that·nearly two-thirds of the office construction permits in the new towns are for speculative buildings rather than for prearranged specific clients, as is more commonly the case elsewhere in the region.

b. Special charges. Firms that have obtained permits to locate in the Paris region must pay a charge. The amount of the charge varies, depending on the location of the firm within the region. For offices, four zones have been established in the region. Zone 1 includes central Paris and most of the near west suburbs. The charge for receiving an office permit is 400 francs per square meter. Zone 2 includes some suburbs to the south and west of zone 1 and La Défense, actually in zone 1 but where new offices are being encouraged. The charge is 300 francs per square meter. The rest of the inner suburbs and some of the western outer suburbs are in zone 3, where the charge is 200 francs per square meter. A few scattered locations within zone 3 have a charge of 100 francs per square meter. Zone 4, the outer suburbs, including all new town land, is not taxed at all (see figure 5–4).[21]

The region is also divided into four zones for charges on new industries. Zone 1 covers a wide area, including all of central Paris and the department of Seine-Saint-Denis, most of Val-de-Marne and Hauts de Seine, and the parts of Yvelines and Val-d'Oise closest to the center. In zone 1 the charge is 150 francs per square meter. Most of the remainder of the region is in zone 2, with a charge of 75 francs per square meter. A few districts on the southern and western fringes of the region comprise zone 3 and have no charge. The five new towns comprise a special fourth zone, where the charge is 25 francs per square meter (see figure 5–5). Thus, the new towns have a charge for industries, but not for offices. This is a reflection of the relative attractiveness of the Paris new towns for industries but not offices.

The seventh plan has an even higher goal of 61.4 percent tertiary-sector jobs between 1976 and 1980. This figure may be realized because a number of office buildings were under construction at the beginning of the seventh plan. Although the new towns failed to achieve the desired percentage of tertiary-sector jobs, they nearly realized the goal for the number of square meters of new office space under construction between 1971 and 1975. The sixth plan called for the initiation of 565,000 square meters, with 427,170 actually begun (75.6 percent of the goal). The figures vary widely among the new

[21]Préfecture de la Région Parisienne, *Région parisienne*, pp. 85–89.

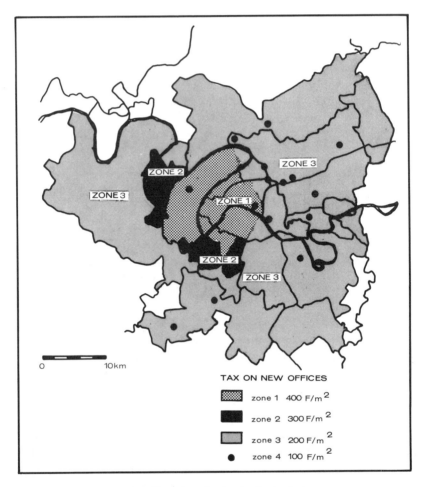

Figure 5–4. Charges for offices locating in the Paris region

towns, with Cergy-Pontoise achieving 150 percent of its goal; Evry 80 percent; Saint-Quentin-en-Yvelines 65 percent; Melun-Sénart 49 percent; and Marne-la-Vallée 0.[22] The relatively strong effort at Cergy-Pontoise and Evry is due to the fact that they have been designated as prefectures for two of the new departments in the Paris region, so that local government offices have been built there.

Pressures on office concentration in central Paris could be alleviated by a policy of encouraging decentralization of existing offices to the new towns. This is rarely done. In reality, the French ministries are the worst offenders of the attitude that location in the center is a

[22] Groupe Central des Villes Nouvelles, *Bilan*, p. 17.

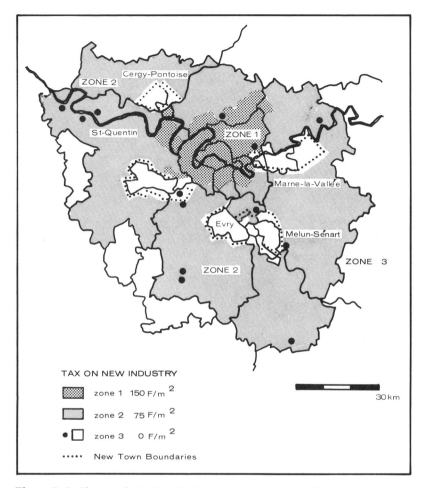

Figure 5–5. Charges for industries locating in the Paris region

prerequisite for maintaining status. The thought of moving out even "nonessential" office jobs is intolerable to the ministries. This attitude contrasts with the situation in Britain, where routine office functions are being moved to new towns. Government agencies in Paris were surveyed a few years ago to examine the possibilities of relocating nonessential personnel, but no ministry agreed. Expansion of government offices in central Paris is almost always approved.[23]

[23]The excuse sometimes given for the inability of planners to secure decentralization agreements from the ministries is that the French administration is not as personnel-heavy as in other countries. The French ministries contain fewer "routine" personnel and are always so understaffed that project funds sometimes have to be used to hire secretaries and other clerical personnel.

Relocation of offices to new towns is also discouraged because the limitation on new office permits in the Paris region covers relocations as well as entirely new businesses. If a firm did want to move to a new town and the annual limit on new offices were exhausted, the firm could not get permission. The theory is that if a firm moves to new offices the old space would be taken over by another firm; the result is therefore a net addition of office space.

The purpose of creating a balance between jobs and residents is to reduce the amount of commuting required. The early results are encouraging. A sample poll in 1975 showed that 59 percent of the residents of four Paris new towns (Melun-Sénart was excluded) worked in the same new town. This figure was confirmed by a more detailed survey at Cergy-Pontoise. That study showed that 49 percent of the residents active in the labor force worked within the new town boundaries, while another 9 percent worked in communes adjacent to the new town. Only 18 percent commuted to central Paris, while the rest worked elsewhere in the region. In contrast, 31 percent of all active residents in the Paris region worked in central Paris and only 37 percent in the same commune as their residence. The figures are even more extreme for the *grands ensembles*: 40 percent of the active residents commuted to central Paris, 40 percent to other parts of the region, and only 20 percent found work in the same commune. Workers at Cergy-Pontoise average only twenty minutes commuting to work compared to over forty minutes among all workers in the region and fifty minutes for suburban workers.[24]

The new towns have achieved a remarkable degree of success in creating a balance between jobs, shops, recreation, and housing, particularly in comparison with the *grands ensembles*. This is due to a conscious effort by the planners to coordinate the rate of attraction of the many elements, while sacrificing the quantitative goals. The Paris new towns have successfully attracted shops and recreation facilities, secondary-sector industries, and lower-income families. The provision of these facilities in the new towns is in sympathy with regional trends and pressures. The problem is in attracting middle-class families and tertiary-sector jobs. The planners have concluded that the best way to attract middle-income residents is by providing office jobs in the new towns. Therefore the pace of development of the new towns is keyed to the rate of attraction of offices. In this way the quantitative impact of the new towns on the distribution of growth is reduced, but the projects are more socially balanced and self-contained than alternative forms of urban development.

[24]Banque National de Paris, Etudes, BNP—Villes Nouvelles, Résultats," mimeographed (Paris: Banque National de Paris, 1977).

INNOVATION IN THE NEW TOWNS

The French new towns are trying to provide an environment superior to the *grands ensembles* through a variety of innovative techniques. Despite the fact that the new towns are not designed primarily as experimental or futuristic communities, they are as close to the perfect laboratory as can be achieved in the day-to-day world. There are virtually no existing residents to object to the introduction of innovative techniques in new towns. The temptation to try out technical innovations is probably as strong today as in Victorian times when many utopian communities were proposed. Contemporary new towns planners must temper their zeal for experimental ideas with sensitivity for hardships that may be imposed on future residents. The innovations must be designed to enhance the product's marketability. In a liberal society, the success of new towns is based in part on individual decisions to move there. The sixth plan stated,

> The new town can be a testing ground in the best sense of the term. In other words, it is not all-permissive, it cannot be the refuge of futurism or utopianism; but precisely because it imposes social, economic, and technical constraints it makes it possible to tackle lucidly and in concrete fashion some of the key problems of urban life in our times.[25]

The most innovative concept in the design of the new towns is the creation of important town centers. The French say they are trying to build "animated" town centers, a concept that corresponds to the French ideal of urban life. The French do not admire the bucolic green image of the British garden city. Their idea of a true city involves a lot of bustle and excitement in a man-made environment. Animated centers are those where a lot of activity takes place. Many people are on the streets performing a variety of roles. All of the major functions in life would be concentrated in the town center including apartments, jobs, and leisure facilities. According to Roullier,

> The aim is to bring together and throw open to each other, in an animated complex, cultural and sports facilities, housing, big stores and small shops, certain forms of handicrafts and services, administration and business. This proximity was common enough in the center of old towns, but is all the more difficult to recreate in a new context since it imposes certain servitudes and since it is necessary to regroup all comers over whom the new town has no direct authority, whose arrival is haphazard, partly unpredictable, and always spread out in time.[26]

To promote integration of all urban functions the EPA's try to cooperate with private developers in the creation of public facilities.

[25] J.-E. Roullier, *French New Towns and Innovation* (Paris: Ministère de l'Aménagement du Territoire, d'Equipement, du Logement, et du Tourisme, 1973), p. 14.
[26] Ibid., p. 8.

Libraries, youth centers, galleries, gyms, and other facilities provided by local authorities are integrated with private enterprise activities such as cinemas, ice rinks, and cafes. In contrast to the rest of the new town, the town center is not privately owned; the EPA retains ownership of the land and leases it to private developers. This arrangement permits the EPA to control the character of the town center — which largely determines the overall visual image of the new town — and to secure much of the profit that accompanies the conversion of rural land for intensive urban use.

The town centers require very complex designs, such as multilevel megastructures. Buildings are joined by pedestrian decks and underground garages. Individual buildings house more than one function. For example, the so-called ''Agora'' at Evry contains the shopping center and community recreational center within the same building (see figure 5–6).

New towns are also ''captors'' of innovative techniques. The former prefect of the Paris region, Maurice Doublet, has called the new towns a testing ground open to all innovations. Several examples can be cited:

1. Public transportation. The new towns have installed a number of innovative devices, such as an electric bus, dial-a-bus, the first fully automated rapid transit line in France, and bus-only lanes. The first new rail line built in France in fifty years was opened in 1975 at Evry. Marne-la-Vallée received a connection to the new Paris regional subway (Réseau Express Régional) in 1977. The other new towns will also soon have new rail lines or RER connections. [27]

2. Pollution control. Research is being undertaken in the new towns to plan for the minimization of pollution. The planners at Le Vaudreuil are trying to provide a nuisance-free town center.

3. Telecommunications. The first domestic use of cable television is planned for the new towns, showing educational and local programs.

---

[27]The most innovative transportation idea was the aerotrain between Cergy-Pontoise and La Défense. The nonstop sixteen-mile trip would have been made in ten minutes, placing downtown Cergy-Pontoise within fifteen minutes of downtown Paris. The aerotrain was originally proposed in the 1960s to connect Orly Airport south of Paris to the new one then under construction at Roissy in the north (Charles de Gaulle Airport). The minister of finance refused to support the project because of a lack of projected patronage but was willing to try it on the Cergy-Pontoise route, where more patronage could be forecast. The Cergy-Pontoise planners embraced the idea. However, by increasing the potential demand the proposed system had to be modified; this modification involved designing larger engines, new track, etc., a process that delayed the project. The aerotrain was finally scrapped in 1974. Instead, Cergy-Pontoise will get a conventional train after several years delay.

Figure 5–6. Evry town center. Much of downtown Evry has now been built. The center includes a shopping center, offices, the prefecture (government offices for the Department of Essonne), a daycare center, a railroad station, and the Agora. The Agora contains a variety of leisure facilities, including an auditorium, swimming pool, cafes, ping-pong tables, a senior citizen center, and a library. (*Techniques & Architecture* No. 301.)

4. Data processing. The use of computers is encouraged in the new towns. The first uses have been to keep track of all underground systems being built and land registration data.

5. Post office. The ministry of posts and telecommunications is attempting to establish new postal delivery networks in the new towns.

6. Electricity. The National Electricity Company is installing the first all-electric heating project in Marne-la-Valleé and L'Isle d'Abeau.

7. Architecture. A number of unusual housing projects have been built in the new towns. Among the notable efforts are a hillside row house project at L'Isle d'Abeau, a large pyramidlike housing project at Evry reminiscent of Moshe Safdie's Habitat, and a Mediterranean-style, pastel-colored rowhouse project at Marne-la-Vallée. Although some of the new towns architecture is not successful, the overall quality is far higher than the *grands ensemble* (see figure 5–7).

The use of new towns as "laboratories of innovation" has apparently been welcomed by the residents. A recent poll discovered that new towns residents considered themselves an elite, occupying a privileged position by virtue of living in a prominent project. They are relatively open to change and in fact welcome it. They are well-informed and supportive of the goals and objectives of the new towns.[28] Approximately three-fourths of the respondents in the survey expressed overall satisfaction with their new town. The figure varied from 85 percent at Evry and 79 percent at Cergy-Pontoise to 69 percent at Marne-la-Vallée and 67 percent at Saint-Quentin-en-Yvelines. The lower rating for the last two is due to the relative lack of community facilities at this point. Whereas 62 percent of the respondents at Evry and 53 percent at Cergy-Pontoise said that the social activities were better than their previous location, only 46 percent at Saint-Quentin-en-Yvelines and 41 percent at Marne-la-Vallée found improvement. However, nearly three-fourths said that their housing was better than their previous residence, including 79 percent at Marne-la-Vallée and 82 percent at Saint-Quentin-en-Yvelines. About one-half thought that working conditions were better in the new towns, with the most favorable aspect being the ease with which a car could be used.

The new towns hope to establish a viable, socially diverse community by encouraging stable tenure. In contrast, many dormitory suburbs serve as staging areas for young families on their way up the social ladder and consequently do not have a strong social foundation.

[28.]Banque National de Paris, "Etudes."

Figure 5–7. Housing in Evry. This housing project, called Evry I, contains both *très-aidé* and *aidé* housing. It is located immediately adjacent to downtown Evry, as can be seen in the background of figure 5–5. The design was the result of an open competition held in the late 1960s. (Etablissement Public de la Ville Nouvelle d'Evry.)

Over two-thirds of the survey respondents indicated that they do not expect to move away from the new town. This is supported by the fact that only 20 percent say they moved to the new towns to secure better housing. About 45 percent came for work-related reasons and 12 percent to be near friends and family. As long as businesses do not move out of the new town — an unlikely occurrence — the residents are likely to stay.

CONCLUSION

I have traced the history of the French new towns policy, the administrative and financial arrangements for implementing the policy, and the quantitative and social achievements. Although the policy is relatively recent in origin useful lessons can be drawn from the experience. For American observers, two lessons are particularly significant. The first lesson concerns the administrative and financial system. As in the United States, France has local authorities and private developers who cannot be ignored in the urban development process. The British-style development corporation is as inappropriate to French as it is to American administrative realities. The French new towns supporters were faced with the task of creating a workable system that preserved the roles of the local authorities and the private sector in the development of nationally financed new towns. Although the precise details of the French solution could not be replicated in the United States, the general principles are clearly relevant.

The French have created new institutions that disturb existing relationships as little as possible. The Etablissement Public d'Aménagement is a public agency with much less power than the British development corporation. It is concerned only with the aspects of new towns development for which local authorities and private developers are clearly unequipped. The French have also solved the local government crisis by coopting the existing local authorities into participating in the new towns development process. The local authorities come together in a union, the Syndicat Communautaire d'Aménagement, which controls the rural areas to be urbanized and leaves alone most of the existing population in the local authorities. The most important function that the SCA performs is the establishment of a uniform tax base within the urbanizing area.

The French have solved one of the major practical problems associated with new towns development in the United States — that new towns are not profitable activities for private developers. The United States has failed to achieve a satisfactory method of supporting the private construction of new towns. Title VII of the 1970 Housing and Urban Development Act authorizes HUD to make loans and guarantees to private developers of new towns. This financial assistance would permit these developers to borrow money below market rates, thereby reducing their carrying charges and consequently the overall project costs. This method proved unsatisfactory when developers began to incur higher expenses than anticipated. Although critics have blamed both the developers and the government for the failures, the real problem is that a new town is much too big for a single private developer to organize.

The French have a more rational method for preserving the profitable participation of private developers in the new towns development process. The EPA acts as the prime developer for the new town. It chops up the new town into a collection of smaller projects that can reasonably be managed by private developers. In this way private developers can achieve profits in their normal manner, while the risks are taken by the only institution large enough to do so—the national government. New towns may or may not be more economical than other projects if all costs of development are compared. The critical point is that their successful realization in a liberal economy depends upon a rational distribution of responsibilities between the public and private sectors based on the strengths and weaknesses of each.

The second lesson for the United States concerns the benefits achieved by the French new towns. They have not succeeded in drastically reorienting the direction of growth in the Paris region. Between 1971 and 1975 the five Paris new towns attracted around 100,000 housing starts, 90,000 residents, and 50,000 jobs. While these are impressive figures, they constitute only some 15–20 percent of the continued growth of the Paris region. The legal and political support is lacking to concentrate a significantly higher percentage of growth in the new towns. In 1965 the Paris new towns were planned to accommodate over three-fourths of the growth of the Paris region until 2000. That figure has steadily declined since the original master plan. In 1971 the sixth plan called for about one-fourth of the growth of the Paris region to be concentrated in the new towns. The seventh plan in 1976 programmed the more realistic figure of 15 percent for the new towns between 1976 and 1980. In effect, the percentage of growth planned for the new towns has declined until it has reached a point comparable to the experience of the London region.

In view of the failure of the new towns in Paris (as in London) to attract more than 15–20 percent of the region's growth, the main benefit of the new towns must be found elsewhere. In fact, the new towns offer a living environment superior to alternative projects. To some extent this is a qualitative judgment but considerable data can be generated to justify it. The major achievement of the French new towns is the creation of socially balanced communities. There is a much greater mixture of different housing types and a balance between residential and nonresidential functions. The new towns, in contrast to other suburban areas, are becoming strong commercial and employment centers. They have much more job opportunities, stores, and recreational facilities than elsewhere in the suburbs. As heterogeneous, self-contained communities the new towns have already made a distinctive contribution to France.

American planners must therefore realize that new towns are not mechanisms for ending all suburban sprawl. They will never succeed in terms of quantitative impact. Rather, new towns are balanced, self-contained communities. A rational new towns policy in the United States can only be based on an understanding that the projects are primarily oriented to achieving social, not quantitative goals.

This evaluation of the French new towns should serve as a beginning rather than a summing up of the understanding of the contributions of new towns to the development of national urban growth policies. The conclusion that the most significant contribution of the French new towns is the creation of socially balanced communities must be further explored. Although we know that the new towns contain a greater mixture of different types of people and functions we don't know the significance of that fact. Information from Britain indicates that their new towns contain a lower incidence of crime, mortality, and health problems than in unplanned cities of similar size. The French new towns are still much too new to permit the compilation of meaningful data. However, the lower level of social disorders could be due to the peculiar characteristics of families attracted (young and mobile) rather than to the socially balanced environment of the new towns. In the United States, new towns could be used to bring together residents of different races as well as different incomes.

This study has raised many questions in addition to answering some. The construction of entirely new towns will always remain one of the most stimulating dreams for urban planners. The French have made the dream a concrete and practical reality.

INDEX

INDEX

161

THE JOHNS HOPKINS UNIVERSITY PRESS

This book was composed in Baskerville Compugraphic text and display by Brushwood Graphics, Inc., from a design by Alan Carter. It was printed on 50-lb. Publishers Eggshell Wove and bound in Joanna Sierra Grande by The Maple Press Company.

Library of Congress Cataloging in Publication Data

Rubenstein, James M.
    The French new towns.

    (Johns Hopkins studies in urban affairs)
    Includes bibliographical references and index.
    1. New towns—France. I. Title.
HT169.F7R8   301.36'3'0944   77–26953
ISBN 0–8018–2104–5

DATE